P9-DMO-577

BenBella

BenBella Books, Inc.
10300 N. Central Expy, Ste 400
Dallas, TX 75231
www.benbellabooks.com
Send feedback to feedback@benbellabooks.com

Printed in the United States of America
10 9 8 7 6 5 4 3 2 1

Library of Congress Cataloging-in-Publication Data is available for this title.
978-1-936661-98-5

Copyediting by Andrea Lynn
Proofreading by Cape Cod Compositors, Inc. and Rainbow Graphics
Cover design by Kit Sweeney
Text design and composition by Kit Sweeney
Printed by Versa Press, Inc.
Except for pages xiv, 58, 69, 73, 83, 193, 209, 235, 247, 255, and 259, food photos by Lindsay Benson Garrett, Manager of Creative Services at Meals On Wheels Association of America.
Photo on page 252 (Bradley Ogden) by Jeremy Ball
Photo on page 118 (Martha Stewart) by Matthew Hranek, courtesy of Martha Stewart Living Omnimedia, Inc.
Photo on page 25 (Suzanne Somers) by Cindy Gold
Photo on page 241 (Alan Muraoka) and 245 (Big Bird) courtesy of Sesame Street® and associated characters, trademarks, service marks and design elements are owned and licensed by Sesame Workshop. © 2011 Sesame Workshop. All Rights Reserved.
Photo on 147 (Mario Batali) by Melanie Dunea
Photo on 174 (Walter Nicholl) by Molly McDonald
Recipe on page 169 (Shrimp Totellini Salad) courtesy of Pete Costalas, cook at Meals On Wheels of Northampton County, Bethlehem, PA

Distributed by Perseus Distribution
(www.perseusdistribution.com)

To place orders through Perseus Distribution:
Tel: 800-343-4499 | Fax: 800-351-5073 | E-mail: orderentry@perseusbooks.com

Significant discounts for bulk sales are available. Please contact Glenn Yeffeth at glenn@benbellabooks.com or (214) 750-3628.

Made With LOVE

The Meals On Wheels Family Cookbook

Edited by Enid Borden

President and CEO of Meals On Wheels Association of America

BenBella Books, Inc.
Dallas, TX

Mom's Green Bean Delight . . . 202

Table of Contents

Main Dishes

Beef

Poultry

Seafood

Vegetable

Casseroles

Pastas and Rice Dishes

Salads

Sides

Desserts

Linguine
with Tomatoes
& Basil . . . 152

Foreword

The world is full of cookbooks. You are holding an unusual one—a cookbook written from the heart by some very special people who, in fact, have enormously generous hearts. This is a book that was indeed Made With Love. The recipes are good-tasting; the personal stories that accompany them are sweet, compelling, funny, and lovingly presented by some of the best people I've ever known. I say that even though so many of them I've never met. But that's what is so special about this book. Through it, we get to meet these folks and hear their stories and discover what joy there is around preparing good food—even just for fun.

Some special folks are sharing these recipes and stories with you because they are committed to helping us raise awareness about the growing issue of senior hunger. We want you to try these recipes and we want you to enjoy them. And when you are doing that, we want you to think about the important role that good food plays in our lives. Then we want you to think about the hundreds of thousands of seniors in America who would not have meals were it not for Meals On Wheels across the country. They are the ones this cookbook is really about. The monies raised from the sale of these books will be used to help us feed hungry seniors in your own communities.

This book truly is a tribute to every mom and dad who raised us; every teacher who taught us; every veteran who fought for us; every farmer who

Grandma's Jell-O . . . 166

tilled the soil for us; and every volunteer who now gives back to them for all they did for us.

Meals On Wheels is a community-based program that reaches millions of people every single day. All who are involved in it—the givers and the receivers—are touched in some way. The simple knock on a door and the delivery of a nutritious meal is a vital lifeline to so many of our neighbors.

The friendly "hello, how ya doing" nature of Meals On Wheels is a welcome reminder to all of us that neighbor helping neighbor is a blessing.

We often say that Meals On Wheels nourishes the soul almost as much as it nourishes the belly. It is absolutely true, and I think this book is testament to that truth. Use these recipes and read the stories and know that you too are helping us in our fight against senior hunger.

Enjoy this book that has been Made With Love and as you sit down to sink your teeth into one of the fabulous dishes, reminisce about your own mealtime conversations with your mom and dad and how special that was. For breaking bread with a loved one is as glorious a celebration as anything I know. The gift of a meal served up with loving hands is priceless.

I have been blessed to work with many wonderful people in my career, but almost every day I meet one more person who will become a hero to me. Who are they? Those big-hearted people who give of their time, talents, resources, and patience to help someone in need are the real heroes in this world. Those who worked so hard to make this book a reality are heroes. And you who have purchased it—well, you are too. You see, you just might have saved a life. You have just made it possible to nourish another person and another soul.

In my family, the kitchen table was always a starting point for new relationships and great conversations. Some of my fondest memories of my mother and father transpired around a three-foot round table filled with good food and much laughter. The world around us was asked to take a break as we indulged our appetites and taste buds for my mother's famous pot roast. Yes, this book is a little reminder to all of us that food should be shared with new friends and old and should be savored with delight; should also be shared with those who are hungry; and most important of all—should be Made With Love.

Enid A. Borden,
President and CEO of Meals On Wheels Association of America

Cherry-Orange Loaf Cake . . . 13

Breakfast

Ann LePage

Ann LePage is the First Lady of Maine. Her husband, Governor Paul LePage, took office in 2011.

Maple Oat Bread

MAKES 1 LOAF

1 c, plus 2 tbsp old-fashioned oats, divided
1 c boiling water
1 (¼-oz) pkg active dry yeast
⅓ c warm water (110°F to 115°F)
½ c maple syrup
2 tsp canola oil
1½ tsp salt
3½ to 4 c all-purpose flour
Canola oil, as needed
1 egg white, lightly beaten

Place 1 cup oats in food processor or blender and process until coarsely chopped. Transfer to a small, heat-proof bowl and add boiling water. Let stand until mixture cools down, registering between 110°F and 115°F.

Meanwhile, in a large mixing bowl, add warm water and sprinkle yeast over it, letting yeast dissolve. Add maple syrup, oil, salt, oat mixture, and 2 cups flour; beat until smooth. Keep stirring, adding enough of the remaining flour until mixture forms a soft dough.

Turn dough onto a lightly floured surface and knead until smooth and elastic, about 6 to 8 minutes.

Lightly grease a large bowl with canola oil, and add dough to it, turning once to coat the surface of the dough. Cover with a dishtowel, and let rise in a warm place until doubled, about 1 hour. After the dough has risen, punch dough down.

Grease a 9-inch round baking dish. Turn dough onto a lightly floured surface, and shape into a 9-inch round loaf. Add dough into the baking dish. Cover again with dishtowel and let rise until doubled again, about 45 minutes.

Preheat oven to 350°F. Brush dough with egg white and sprinkle with remaining 2 tablespoons oats. Bake until golden brown, about 30 to 35 minutes. Remove bread from pan onto a wire rack and cool.

I found this recipe in a Light & Tasty *magazine years ago and have made it for my family ever since. My children would sit at the kitchen counter and wait for it to cool down to enjoy their first slice. I, on the other hand, couldn't wait and had to eat it right from the oven.*

K C Baking Powder Biscuits

MAKES ABOUT 20 BISCUITS

4 c pastry flour or cake flour
4 tsp baking powder, like K C Baking Powder
1 tsp salt
¼ c shortening
About 1½ c milk or water, as needed

Preheat oven to 400°F.

In a bowl, add flour, baking powder, and salt. Sift the ingredients together three times.

Add the shortening, and use the tips of your fingers to work the shortening into the flour until the mixture resembles coarse crumbs.

Gradually add milk or water until a soft dough forms. Turn dough onto a lightly-floured surface and knead lightly just until dough comes together.

Roll dough out until it is ¼-inch thick. Use a 3-inch biscuit or round cookie cutter to cut dough into rounds. Place on ungreased baking sheet and bake until golden brown, about 12 to 15 minutes.

Carol Mead

Carol Mead is the First Lady of Wyoming. Her husband, Governor Matt Mead, took office in 2011.

I am very happy to share with Meals On Wheels a story that was written by my mother about how in the early 1940s on her ranch in southern Idaho, she became the baking powder biscuit queen—without anyone knowing the secret ingredient that made her biscuits so light:

My mother was an excellent cook. She could make biscuits, rolls, bread and pancakes with sourdough. Sourdough had to be mixed the night before to have enough time to ferment. But sometimes, it didn't get mixed the night before. On such occasions, baking powder biscuits were quick and handy. Mother's biscuits were not light and fluffy but rather small and hard. The reason being that my mother, and father too, had a notion that baking powder was unhealthy—something in it was hard on the stomach. Hence, Mother could not bring herself to put more than one teaspoon of baking powder in anything she made.

When I was old enough to make things on my own I discovered the recipe for biscuits on the baking powder can. It was using this recipe that made my biscuits always turn out well. I guarded my secret. This recipe called for four teaspoons of baking powder in two cups of flour. My mother did not ask questions because she was happy to turn over any cooking or baking to me that I was able to do. She let me make the biscuits when needed.

In 1945, Mother had an extended stay in the hospital with a bout of corneal ulcers. When she came home, she was legally blind. I came home from school to help out while she was adjusting to her lack of sight. One day, I was in the kitchen preparing our dinner, thinking gloomy thoughts about how we would manage and how much I would miss my mother's comments about what she saw. Mother was in her room adjacent to the kitchen, likely thinking similar thoughts, when all at once she called out "Joy!! You put four teaspoons of baking powder in the biscuits!!" This startled me. I composed myself for a second and then asked, "Mother, how do you know what I'm doing? You're not even in the same room."

She replied, "I heard you scraping the spoon on the side of the can!" My secret was out. To my parents, my biscuits were never as good as they had been, but this episode did much to allay my fears about my mother's ability to cope. When she had her sight, she had never figured out why my baking powder biscuits were better than hers.

Joan Rivers

The iconic funny woman Joan Rivers is currently best known for her E! red carpet commentary with daughter Melissa.

For more than twenty years, this has been my favorite recipe to make for family and friends. I used to make it for my daughter, Melissa. Now I make it for my grandson Cooper and it's great to see it transcend the generations. For holidays and special occasions, raisin bread may be substituted but follow the same procedure. For these special occasions we call it "Joan Rivers' Holiday Toast."

Joan Rivers' Toast

MAKES 2

2 slices white bread
Butter or margarine, as needed

Take 2 slices of white bread.

Place them in a toaster.

Press down the handle.

Wait 2 minutes or until toast pops up.

Spread butter over slices after removing them from the toaster.

STEVEN L. BESHEAR

Steve Beshear is the governor of Kentucky, having previously served in the Kentucky House of Representatives and as the state's attorney general and lieutenant governor.

Spoon Cornbread

MAKES 8 TO 10 SERVINGS

2¼ c milk
2 tbsp butter, plus more to serve
1 tsp salt
⅔ c yellow cornmeal
3 eggs, separated

Preheat oven to 375°F. Grease an 8- by 10-inch baking dish.

In a medium pot, add milk and butter, and bring to a boil over high heat. Stir in the salt and cornmeal, and cook for 1 minute. Remove from heat and set aside to cool for 5 minutes. Whisk egg yolks into the cooled cornmeal.

Meanwhile, add egg whites to a large bowl, and beat with a hand mixer until stiff peaks form. Then, gently fold egg whites into cornmeal mixture.

Pour batter into the prepared baking dish and bake until cornbread is set in the center and lightly browned on top, about 35 minutes. Serve warm, scooped out of the baking dish with lots of butter.

This is the spoon cornbread recipe that many generations of mothers in my family have used, and that we continue to use for family functions at the Governor's Mansion. Jane and I hope you enjoy this wonderful dish as much as we do.

John Kitzhaber

John Kitzhaber is the governor of Oregon, serving from 1995 – 2003 and 2010 – present.

Kuchen (German Coffee Cake)

SERVES 24

¼ c warm water (110°F to 115°F)
2 (¼-oz) pkg active dry yeast
2 c milk
1 c water
1 tbsp salt
1 c sugar
½ c shortening or margarine, melted
3 large eggs, lightly beaten
2 c raisins
8 to 9 c flour, divided
Oil, as needed
1½ tsp ground cinnamon

In a small heat-proof bowl, add warm water and sprinkle yeast over it, letting yeast dissolve.

Meanwhile, in a heavy-duty large pot, add milk and warm over medium-high heat, just until tiny bubbles form around the edge of the pot. Remove from heat and stir in the water, salt, sugar, and shortening.

Continue adding ingredients into the pot—stirring in dissolved yeast, beaten eggs, raisins and 4 cups flour. Add remaining 4 to 5 cups of flour, 1 cup at a time, mixing well after each addition, until mixture forms a soft dough.

Turn dough onto a lightly-floured surface and knead until dough is smooth and pliable. Lightly grease a large bowl with oil, and add dough. Cover bowl with a dishtowel and let dough rise until doubled in size, up to 1 hour. Punch dough down and knead again until smooth. Shape dough into 3- to 4-inch balls and place in 3 greased 9-inch cake pans. Let dough rise until doubled in size, about 30 minutes.

Preheat oven to 350°F. Brush dough lightly with water and sprinkle with cinnamon. Place cake pans in preheated oven, and bake bread until golden brown, about 30 to 40 minutes.

I may not be the world's best cook, but I certainly appreciate good, healthy food. My favorites are those made with Oregon-grown fruits and vegetables, dairy products, and grains. I am happy to share my recipe for "Kuchen," a recipe from my great-grandmother that has been handed down through four generations.

My maternal grandmother grew up on a farm in southern Illinois. She was one of twelve children in a time when big families on farms were common then, even necessary, because enough hands were needed to make sure everything got done.

Still, my grandmother loved farm life. As a young woman, she was shipped off to St. Louis to make her way in the big city. And she did, becoming a seamstress in the city's then bustling garment district along Washington Avenue. But whenever she started telling stories, they were invariably about life on the farm. To my young city boy ears, none of these stories made me feel that I had missed out on anything by not growing up on a farm. They ranged from slightly dull to downright horrifying.

One story, though, stuck with me and changed in meaning as I heard it over the years. Not so much a story, really—just a fact remembered from my grandmother's childhood which she shared during each Christmas holiday without fail. With twelve siblings and the no-nonsense approach to life that farm-living demands, Christmas was not the orgy of presents all too common these days. There were dolls, tops, hair ribbons and at least one child-sized wagon or sleigh, but these were not the gifts my grandmother spoke of about Christmas on the farm. The gift she remembered—something each family member got every year, but only at Christmas—was a fresh orange.

She never said so, but I'm guessing the oranges she remembered were not the juicy, seedless navel beauties we buy by the bagful whenever the mood strikes us. Still, to the young farm girl like my grandmother, these once-a-year treats were exotic—magical even, having traveled an unimaginable distance from some unknown land.

Filtered through my young, urban ears, this story made my grandmother's farm life seem utterly impoverished, gray and bereft of even the simplest of pleasures. It was only later as an adult, long after my grandmother had passed away, that I understood the look in her eyes, the softening of her features, as she recounted the glory of those oranges every year. Even now, with our global reach giving us oranges stacked high in the supermarket year round, how can you not respond to the simple pleasure of tearing into the peel of an orange, having its bright fragrance wrap around you, and linger on your hands? Now imagine having this experience only once a year.

I created this Cherry-Orange Loaf Cake to honor the memory of a simple Christmas gift that meant so much to my grandmother—an orange. My grandmother was also a big fan of stollens, coffee cakes and gooey butter cakes, a St. Louis delicacy. More Saturdays than not, treats like these would make their way into our house, usually from the favorite bakery on Cherokee Street. Some were sugary sweet, but as often they would be dense, non-cakey loaves with just a little sweetness that went perfect with a cup of coffee. This Cherry-Orange Loaf Cake is that kind of dessert—not overly sweet and, while not exactly dense, not exactly fluffy either. Cherries, chopped pecans and flaxseed meal give it a satisfying textural richness while a drizzle of orange-enhanced frosting adds a fresh citrus finish, just perfect to serve for the holidays.

Terry Boyd

Terry Boyd is the author of Blue Kitchen, a food blog for home cooks, and his recipes have appeared in the *Chicago Sun-Times*, *Bon Appetit*, and *Saveur*.

Cherry-Orange Loaf Cake

SERVES 12

FOR THE CAKE:
¼ c vegetable oil, plus more to grease pan
1 c plus 1 tbsp granulated sugar, divided
2 c all-purpose flour
6 tbsp flaxseed meal (or 3 tbsp flaxseed ground in small food processor)
1½ tsp baking powder
½ tsp baking soda
½ tsp salt
¾ c low-fat buttermilk
Zest of 1 orange
1 tsp vanilla extract
2 large eggs
1 c dried cherries, rehydrated in boiling water for 20 minutes and drained
¼ c chopped pecans

FOR THE FROSTING:
½ c confectioners' sugar
1 tbsp freshly squeezed orange juice

Preheat oven to 350°F. Prepare a 4- by 8-inch loaf pan by coating with oil. Add 1 tablespoon of sugar, and shake to coat the pan evenly. Reserve until needed.

In a medium bowl, add flour, flaxseed meal, baking powder, baking soda, and salt, stirring well to combine ingredients.

In a small bowl, add ¼ cup oil, buttermilk, orange zest, and extract, and mix to combine.

In a large bowl, combine remaining 1 cup sugar with eggs. Use an electric mixer, and beat at high speed until mixture has thickened and turned pale yellow, about 3 minutes. Add one-third of the flour mixture, beat until blended, one-half the buttermilk mixture, beat until blended, and continue until all the flour and buttermilk mixtures have been combined. Stir cherries and pecans into batter, mixing to distribute evenly.

Pour batter into the prepared pan and bake for 55 minutes, or until a wooden pick inserted in center comes out clean. Let cool for 5 minutes. Then, use a baking spatula to loosen cake frm the edges of the pan. Remove cake from the pan, and let cool completely on a wire rack.

Once cake is completely cool, begin making the frosting: Sift confectioners' sugar into a small bowl, and add orange juice, whisking to combine. Using a spoon, drizzle the frosting over the top of the cake, letting it run down the side of the loaf.

Jack Jones

Jack Jones is a Grammy-winning singer, known for his songs "Wives and Lovers," "Lollipops and Roses," "Call Me Irresponsible," and "The Love Boat Theme." He also appeared on variety shows, such as *The Ed Sullivan Show*, *American Bandstand*, and *The Andy Williams Show*.

Pancake Soufflé

SERVES 6 TO 8

2 tbsp butter, softened
4 eggs
2 c milk or soy milk
1 c flour
2 tbsp sugar
1 tsp vanilla extract
Pinch of salt
Maple syrup, as needed

Preheat oven to 450°F. Grease a 9- by 11- by 3-inch Pyrex® dish with butter.

In a large bowl, add eggs, and whisk together in a large bowl. Gradually whisk in milk, flour, sugar, vanilla and salt, and continue whisking until batter is smooth.

Pour the batter into the prepared baking dish and place on the middle rack. Bake 20 to 25 minutes until soufflé is puffed and golden. Remove from oven, and serve immediately drizzled with maple syrup.

In today's world, there is little or no chance to fully communicate with one another, other than using fragmented bits of high-speed electronic data like a text or e-mail. These messages, more often than not, have the human emotions, or lack thereof, filtered out or misunderstood. (One day, I wrote an e-mail in all caps and was accused of yelling.) A good old-fashioned family meal is the ultimate opportunity for mutual understanding.

When a family sits down to a meal, and they have the discipline to cut off all superficial conduits to the outside world, they are focused on each other's subtle needs, such as love, forgiveness, and humor. There was a time, say back in the days of Abraham Lincoln, when one of the discussions at the dinner table might have been about how one's daughter was impatiently waiting for a long overdue letter from her boyfriend. But in today's enabling world, she might be impatiently staring at the screen of her phone that is lying next to her glass of milk and saying nothing—long live the family meal—especially breakfast—with this Pancake Soufflé.

Mess Hall Dip . . . 19

Appetizers

Amy Reed and Amanda Plotnicki

Amy Reed of Fort Worth, Texas has been blissfully married for 18 years, with three step-children and two grandchildren. She is a committee member of Meals On Wheels of Tarrant County Annual Casino Night and Co-Chair of the MOW 2012 High Heels for Hot Meals Luncheon.

Amanda Plotnicki is a supporter to MOW of Tarrant County. She has been married for 38 years, and mother of Amy Reed and Ben III.

Christmas Morning Cheese Stuff

SERVES 10

1 (32-oz) block Velveeta® cheese, cubed
1 (12-oz) tube ground sausage, cooked and drained
1 (5-oz) small jar green olives with pimentos, sliced
1 loaf Pepperidge Farm Rye® or Pumpernickel Party Bread

In a large heat-proof container, add Velveeta cubes, and warm until melted. Stir in cooked sausage and olives, mixing well.

Place in a warming dish or a slow cooker. Serve on bread.

Besides waking up at the crack of dawn out of excitement to open gifts from Santa, my stomach couldn't wait to eat my most favorite thing in the world—my mother's Christmas Morning Cheese Stuff. Every year she had this ready for us on Christmas morning, and the tradition still continues. Plus, this makes a great appetizer year-round. Enjoy!

Sgt. Slaughter

Sgt. Slaughter is a former WWE professional wrestler whose professional persona has been incorporated into comic books, animated series, and toy lines.

Mess Hall Dip

From *Can You Take the Heat?: The WWF is Cooking!* (William Morrow, 2000)

SERVES 10 TO 12

1 tsp olive oil
1 tsp butter
1 lb ground sirloin or ground turkey
Salt to taste
½ tsp garlic salt
3 (15-oz) cans Hormel® Chili No Beans
1 (8-oz) pkg cream cheese, cut into pieces
1 c shredded mild cheddar cheese
Sugar, to taste

In a large skillet over medium-high heat, warm oil and butter. Add ground meat, garlic salt, salt, and pepper. Cook, stirring occasionally, until meat is cooked through, about 10 minutes.

Remove skillet from heat, and drain the oil from the meat. Add chili to meat, and warm mixture over medium-high heat. Stir in the cream cheese and once melted, add the cheddar cheese. Season to taste with the sugar, salt, and pepper, and serve.

This is my mom's chili recipe minus the beans. However, I added some other ingredients to turn it into a dip. I serve it with all different types of chips like corn chips, Fritos,® Ruffles,® and blue corn tortilla chips. I like this recipe because it's great for watching Monday Night RAW; *plus, it's almost a meal in itself.*

Shirley Jones and Marty Ingels

Shirley Jones is an Academy-Award winning actress and singer, known for her role as Shirley Partridge on *The Partridge Family*.

Marty Ingels is an actor and comedian, who played a recurring role on *The Dick Van Dyke Show* and is best known for his voice-over work in cartoons and commercials.

Nutty Cheese Roll

SERVES 16

1 (8-oz) pkg fat-free cream cheese, softened
1 oz blue cheese, crumbled
½ c shredded fat-free cheddar cheese
¼ tsp garlic powder
1 tbsp brandy
1 tbsp sherry
½ tsp Worcestershire sauce
⅛ tsp ground white pepper
½ c finely chopped toasted walnuts
½ c finely chopped toasted almonds
Crackers, toast points, or baguette slices, to serve

In a large bowl, combine all the ingredients, except nuts. Stir until evenly mixed.

Add nuts to a large plate, gently stirring to mix nuts together.

Shape cheese into a ball and roll in nuts until thoroughly covered. Wrap cheese ball tightly with plastic wrap and refrigerate for at least 2 hours.

Serve cheese ball with crackers, toast points or baguette slices.

They say that the virtue of sitting down as a family gives you the opportunity to share the events of your day and to bond as a family. Start the meal with this Nutty Cheese Roll.

TARA FUNK

Tara Funk is a long-time volunteer, delivering meals to seniors for Meals On Wheels in Cleveland, Ohio.

Mexican Pinwheels

SERVES 10 TO 12

2 (8-oz) pkg cream cheese, softened
1 c salsa, plus more as needed
1½ c shredded cheddar cheese
8 to 10 flour tortillas

In a large bowl, add cream cheese, salsa, and cheddar, and mix together until well combined.

Divide the mixture evenly between the tortillas, spreading a thin layer onto each tortilla. Roll the filled tortillas up as tightly as possible, and then use a serrated knife to cut into approximately 1-inch sections.

Refrigerate pinwheels until serving time, and serve with additional salsa for dipping.

The gratitude, kindness, and smiles that I receive from the seniors have kept me volunteering for Meals On Wheels for more than three years. I'm always amazed at how friendly and welcoming they are in spite of their many health issues. These folks really help me to remember what's important in life—family, friendships, and service to others who need it. With shrinking state dollars and pensions, coupled by rapidly aging baby boomers, I believe it is more crucial than ever to continue the Meals On Wheels' mission. Our seniors deserve it.

We chose this recipe to share because it's a quick and easy favorite that was introduced to us by my mom, both perfect for kids' parties and grown-up get-togethers. It's also simple enough for kids to make themselves, which is always fun.

Charles Grodin

Charles Grodin is an actor, comedian, and author. He's best known for his work in *The Heartbreak Kid* and *Midnight Run*.

Fried Chicken Wings

SERVES 1

Canola oil, as needed
Chicken wings, as needed

Warm canola oil into the electric frying pan. Add chicken wings, and fry until done.

Growing up in Pittsburgh, Pennsylvania, in the 1940s and 50s, my family would always have dinner together. My dad sat where he felt was the head of the table in our kitchen, where dinner was usually served. The problem was the chair at the head of the table in the kitchen had to often be moved during dinner to get into the refrigerator. My dad was annoyed by this moving of his chair throughout dinner, but chose to remain in that seat. "What? What is it?" I remember him asking.

It was a happy time. I don't remember my mother ever serving chicken wings, but when I first came to New York at twenty years old, that's what I mostly ate. Chicken wings were nineteen cents a package, and that's what I could afford. I lived in Room 410 in the Capitol Hall Hotel on West 87th Street. The rent was ten dollars a week. My room had no window and no bathroom (There was a bathroom in the hall that I shared with sixteen or so other tenants.). There was no stove and no hot plate allowed, which, of course, meant no cooking allowed. Because I couldn't afford to eat in a restaurant, I bought an electric frying pan, which I slipped in under my coat to cook my chicken wings. My mentee, Alex Fischetti, once asked me since I've always said I don't lie—"Wasn't that a lie?" I said it would be a lie—if anyone ever asked me if I cooked in my room—which no one did. I told Alex that I felt if it went to court, I'd be found not guilty. Alex asked, "On what grounds?" I told him, "Need to eat."

Capitol Hall Hotel has since been upgraded to a homeless shelter.

SUZANNE SOMERS

Suzanne Somers is an actress and author. Known for her roles on *Three's Company* and *Step by Step*, Somers has also written several bestselling self help books.

Bruschetta Artichokes

From *The Sexy Forever Recipe Bible* (Three Rivers Press, Random House, 2011)

SERVES 4

Juice of 1 lemon
4 large artichokes
3 ripe tomatoes, chopped
1 bunch fresh basil, chopped
¼ c extra-virgin olive oil
Salt and ground black pepper

Fill a large bowl with water, and add lemon juice. One at a time, trim the artichokes by using a serrated knife to cut off the tops of the inedible, prickly outer leaves, barely exposing the purple center of the choke. Trim the tips from the remaining leaves using scissors. Place each prepared artichoke in the bowl of lemon water to prevent discoloration.

Fill a large pot with 4 inches of water. Add the artichokes into a steamer basket and place into the pot. Bring water to a boil over high heat, and then reduce heat to low so liquid is simmering. Cover with a lid, and steam artichokes until tender, about 40 to 60 minutes depending on the artichoke size. Remove from steamer, and let cool.

When cool, use a spoon to scoop out the inedible, hairy chokes, being careful to keep the remaining bottom of the artichoke—known as the artichoke heart—intact.

In a medium bowl, combine tomatoes, basil, olive oil, salt, and pepper, and toss to combine. Spoon the tomato mixture into the center of the artichokes and serve.

One of the great joys of my life is my organic garden. Alan and I walk down each day and "pick" our meals. Here's a lovely recipe for a beautiful artichoke—it's bruschetta without the bread! Recipe from The Sexy Forever Recipe Bible *by Suzanne Somers, published by Three Rivers Press, a division of Random House, Inc., 2011.*

Amy Winter

Amy Winter is the Executive Vice President and General Manager of TLC for the Discovery Communications network.

Dabney's Cucumber Dip

SERVES 6

1 (16-oz) container sour cream
3 tbsp finely chopped English cucumber
2 tbsp finely chopped chives
2 tbsp finely chopped tarragon
Salt and ground black pepper, to taste
Pita chips, crackers, bread, or an assortment of dipping vegetables, to serve

In a medium bowl, add sour cream, cucumber, chives, and tarragon. Stir together to combine, and season to taste with salt and pepper.

Chill until ready to serve. Serve with accompaniments.

My favorite thing to make is dip because it usually means that family and friends are coming over to leisurely visit and relax. And let's be honest, dip is usually easy and quick to make. This particular recipe I learned from a dear friend (and mother of triplets!) while we were on a beach trip. I was stunned that she could make it without looking at a recipe. (She's equally amazed by my specialty drink-making skills, but that's for another book.) This cucumber dip is light, summery, and equally good on a pita chip or a dipping veggie—and it takes me right back to that perfectly wonderful vacation I'll always remember.

This antipasto dish is heavenly. This is the mother lode—I have seen people go into a trance over this dish, even people who would swear they don't eat anchovies. Bagna Cauda is a peasant dish from the Piedmont region in Northern Italy, the same region that gives us Barbaresco and Barolo. Ideally, you make this in an earthenware pot and have a fondue pot warmer, like the canned heat of a Sterno, on the table so that the bagna cauda stays warm. If you have an old fondue pot from the 70s, that'll work too. If not, this is a great reason to get one. Cooks disagree as to the ratio of oil to butter in the sauce; it seems to depend on what village you come from. Personally, I think the butter should be subservient to the oil, but present, because it adds a nice nuttiness to the sauce. Don't forget to put out crusty bread for dipping, and I like this served with Prosecco or Champagne.

Jill Eikenberry and Michael Tucker

Jill Eikenberry and Michael Tucker are actors, best known for their roles on *L.A. Law*. Eikenberry won a Golden Globe award for her role on the show and has also appeared on *Numb3rs*, *Law & Order*, *Judging Amy*, and *Strong Medicine*. In addition to acting, Tucker is also the author of three books and writes the food and travel blog, Notes From the Culinary Wasteland.

Peperoni in Bagna Cauda
(Roasted Peppers in Hot Anchovy Sauce)

SERVES 4 TO 6

4 red or yellow bell peppers, stems trimmed
¾ c olive oil
4 tbsp butter
4 cloves garlic, minced
10 canned salt-packed anchovies, rinsed and finely-chopped
Salt, to taste
Baguette or toast points, to serve

Make the peppers: To roast in the broiler, preheat broiler. Place peppers on a baking sheet and cook in the preheated broiler until the skin blackens and chars, turning peppers to ensure even charring on all sides. To use the stovetop, place one or two peppers on a gas burner over high heat, cooking until skin blackens and chars. When peppers are charred, transfer to a bowl and cover tightly with plastic wrap. Let sit for 10 to 15 minutes.

When peppers are cool enough to handle, peel off the charred skins, and cut away the seeds and ribs. Cut peppers into bite-size pieces.

Make the sauce: In a sauce pan, add oil and butter, and warm over low heat until butter melts. Add garlic and cook until aromatic (without browning), just 30 seconds or so. Add anchovies, stirring until anchovies dissolve into the oil mixture. Add a pinch of salt to taste, and keep mixture warm over low heat.

To serve, arrange peppers on a platter, along with bread. Pour sauce into a small fondue pot or bowl. Dip peppers into sauce and serve with bread.

Jill Smith

Jill Smith is a caseworker for Lifescape Community Services, an Illinois agency that serves the needs of older adults and offers Meals On Wheels services.

Crab Cheesecake

SERVES 12

1 c buttery crackers, like Ritz®, crushed
3 tbsp melted butter
1 c finely chopped pecans or almonds (optional)
2 (8-oz) pkg cream cheese, at room temperature
3 large eggs
¾ c sour cream, divided
1 tsp lemon juice
1 tbsp grated onion
¼ tsp Old Bay® seasoning
2 drops Tabasco® sauce, or to taste
⅛ tsp ground black pepper
1 c canned lump crabmeat
Pita chips or crackers, to serve

Preheat the oven to 350°F. In a medium bowl, mix together cracker crumbs, butter, and (optional) nuts. Spread the mixture evenly on the bottom of a 9-inch springform pan. Bake for about 10 minutes until golden. Remove from oven, and set aside to cool.

Reduce oven heat to 325°F.

In a large bowl, add cream cheese, eggs, and ¼ cup sour cream. Using an electric mixer, beat mixture until fluffy. Add the lemon juice, onion, Old Bay, Tabasco, pepper, and crabmeat, stirring with a spatula to incorporate into mixture. Pour into the cooled crust and bake 50 minutes until the filling sets.

Remove from the oven. Run a knife around the edge of the cake, loosening it from the pan. Cool crab cheesecake on a wire rack, remove the sides of the pan when cooled. Spread the top of the cake with remaining ½ cup sour cream, and chill. Serve with desired crackers.

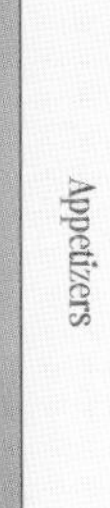

This appetizer makes a delicious spread for any occasion that can be served with your favorite crackers or pita chips.

Susan Orlean

Susan Orlean is a journalist who has written for *The New Yorker*, *Vogue*, *Rolling Stone*, and *Esquire*.

Sugar & Spice Baked Shrimp

SERVES 4

1 c sugar
2½ tsp kosher salt
½ tsp ground black pepper
1 large clove garlic, minced
1 (1½-inch) piece gingerroot, minced
½ tsp cayenne powder
½ tsp ground allspice
¼ tsp turmeric
2 tbsp flour
Oil, as needed
24 to 36 raw shrimp, peeled with tails left on
1 lime, cut in half

In a large bowl, combine all ingredients, except oil, shrimp, and lime, whisking until well-mixed. (This can be done several hours ahead of time.)

When ready to bake, preheat oven to 500°F and grease a baking sheet lightly with oil.

Dredge shrimp in the sugar and spice mixture, shaking off excess spices. Place coated shrimp on baking sheet in an even layer.

Bake shrimp in preheated oven until shrimp is cooked through and the sugar begins to caramelize, about 8 to 10 minutes, keeping a careful watch to make sure the sugar doesn't burn.

Remove shrimp from oven and use a spatula to transfer and arrange onto a serving platter. Garnish shrimp with lime juice and serve immediately.

I first met these shrimp in a Manhattan apartment on a windy night in March. They were being passed around as appetizers, and I took one, expecting very little; I've just had too many shrimp appetizers in my time to find any of them very intriguing. As I recall, I was mid-sentence with a distinguished guest when I first took a bite. Suddenly, I couldn't hear a word the distinguished guest was saying— I was completely distracted by the incredible sweet, spicy taste of this shrimp. As soon as I finished, I hunted down the server and scooped up as many more shrimp as I could. I seem to recall the distinguished guest watched me rush away with a look that was somewhere between wounded and irate. What could I do? I was smitten by the shrimp. I wouldn't leave the apartment until the hostess, Jane, gave me the recipe, and I've made it dozens of times since. I suggest doubling the recipe, because you will want many, many more than one serving.

New Mexican Green Chile & Pork Stew . . . 56

Soups and Stews

Denise Morrison

Denise Morrison is the President and CEO of Campbell Soup Company, formerly working for major brands including Kraft Foods, Proctor & Gamble, Pepsi-Cola, and Nabisco.

Red Devil

SERVES 4

3 tbsp butter
1 (16-oz) block Velveeta® cheese, cut into ½-inch cubes
1 (10¾-oz) can Campbell's® Condensed Tomato Soup
4 slices white bread, toasted and cut in half diagonally

Prepare a double boiler by adding 2 inches of water to the bottom half of a double boiler. Bring water to a boil over medium-high heat.

Melt butter in the top half of the double boiler. Add Velveeta cubes, letting melt with butter, and stirring to combine until smooth. Add soup, and stir until creamy and smooth. Cover, and remove from heat.

In a shallow bowl or on a plate, add 2 toast points. Pour ½ cup of sauce over toast and serve immediately.

Denise Morrison's favorite childhood recipe is "Red Devil." Her mother served it every Friday during Lent. "It was a real treat," she said.

Dr. Ruth

Ruth Westheimer is a psychosexual therapist who pioneered speaking frankly about sexual matters on radio and television and in her popular column, "Ask Dr. Ruth."

Chicken Soup

SERVES 6 TO 8

1 (5- to 6-lb) chicken, cut into quarters
6 to 7 quarts cold water, or more if necessary
1 medium onion, quartered
3 medium carrots, peeled and cut in chunks
2 stalks celery with leaves, cut in chunks
3 medium parsnips or 1 small celery root, peeled and cut into chunks
3 sprigs parsley
Salt and ground black pepper, to taste
Egg noodles, cooked rice or matzo balls, to serve (optional)

In a large stockpot, add chicken and fill with enough water to fully cover the chicken pieces. Bring to a boil over high heat. Once boiling, reduce heat to low, and simmer broth for about 1 hour. Using a skimmer or slotted spoon, occasionally remove scum as it forms on the soup surface.

Add the onion, carrots, celery, parsnips (or celery root), and parsley into the pot, and continue to simmer for 1 more hour. Remove chicken and vegetables from broth, reserving chicken for another use and vegetables to return to soup.

Cool soup, and chill in the refrigerator until the fat solidifies on the surface. Use a spoon to skim fat from the soup. Return the degreased soup to pot, and warm over medium heat. Stir in the reserved vegetables, and season with salt and pepper. Serve on its own, or with noodles, rice, or matzo balls.

It is said that chicken soup has healing powers—it cures colds, the flu, and all kind of ailments. I would like to believe this is true. My favorite way to serve this soup is to purée the cooked vegetables in a blender or food processor until smooth, and stir it into the soup before serving for a nice creamy texture.

My mother was never interested in cooking. "I couldn't boil an egg, when I married your father," she once confessed. As a result, my sisters and I became foodies. Then, two of us married men who love to cook. These days with my husband, I do the cleaning and help with menu planning and preparation, while he does most of the cooking. On the rare occasion that I do cook, I fall back on timeless recipes from my Southern upbringing. (Yes, I can make fried chicken to die for.) My husband, Chris, on the other hand, is a fearless cook and will go to all ends of the earth for a good recipe. He recently found a West African Peanut Soup with Chicken recipe in the New York Times. *We tried it, then tweaked it a little to make it our own. This adapted recipe has since become a favorite that we love to share with friends.*

Marshall Chapman

Marshall Chapman is an author and singer-songwriter whose songs have been recorded by artists such as Jimmy Buffett, Wynonna, and Olivia Newton-John.

West African Peanut Soup with Chicken

SERVES 6 TO 8

2 tbsp peanut or canola oil
1 medium red or white onion, chopped
1 tbsp minced fresh ginger
1 tbsp minced garlic
½ lb boneless, skinless chicken thighs, cut into 1-inch pieces
¾ c roasted roughly chopped peanuts, divided
Pinch of cayenne powder
Salt and ground black pepper, to taste
6 c chicken or vegetable stock
2 sweet potatoes or yams (about 1 lb), peeled and cut into thick slices
8 plum tomatoes, cored and halved
½ lb kale, washed and cut into wide ribbons
¼ to ½ c chunky or smooth peanut butter

Heat oil in a deep skillet or medium saucepan over medium heat. Add onion, ginger, and garlic, and cook, stirring occasionally, until onion is soft, 3 to 5 minutes. Add chicken and continue cooking for another 3 or 4 minutes, until the chicken starts to brown.

Add ½ cup peanuts, cayenne, salt, and pepper to the mixture. Stir in the stock and the sweet potatoes, and bring to a boil. Once boiling, reduce heat to medium-low so the soup simmers. Stir in tomatoes and kale, then cook, stirring occasionally, until chicken is cooked through and greens are soft, about 20 minutes.

Stir in ¼ cup peanut butter. Taste, adjust seasoning (you may want to add more peanut butter at this point) and serve, garnished with remaining peanuts.

Ricky Skaggs

Ricky Skaggs is a Grammy Award-winning country and bluegrass musician, producer, and composer.

Chicken Pickin' Corn Soup

SERVES 6 TO 8

1 tbsp vegetable oil
1 tbsp McCormick's® Chicken Seasoning
Salt and ground black pepper, to taste
4 boneless, skinless chicken breasts, cut into 1-inch pieces
1 (10.7-oz) can cream of chicken soup
1 (10.7-oz) can cream of mushroom soup
2¼ c water, divided
4 medium potatoes, cut into 1-inch pieces
2 medium onions, chopped
1 (15.2-oz) can whole kernel corn, drained
1 (15.2-oz) can cream-style corn
1½ tbsp cornstarch

Heat oil in large, heavy-bottomed pot over medium-high heat. Season chicken with seasoning, and add to oil. Cook, stirring occasionally, until chicken is evenly browned and cooked through. Use a slotted spoon to remove chicken from pot and reserve.

Add soups and 1¼ cups water to pot and bring to a boil over high heat. Stir in potatoes, onions, and both canned corns. Bring soup to a boil and return chicken to pot.

In a small bowl, add cornstarch and 1 cup of water, whisking together to combine. Add cornstarch mixture to the soup. Cover soup with a lid, and reduce heat to medium-low. Simmer soup for 45 minutes to 1 hour, stirring occasionally, to prevent sticking.

Season soup to taste, and serve.

I was in a hurry and got to messin' around in the kitchen of what to put together to eat. With the ingredients I already had on hand, it came to me to combine a couple of different recipes together to make this tasty soup. My idea to brown the chicken and then add it to the corn adds tremendous flavor.

Robert Egger

Robert Egger is the president of DC Central Kitchen, which provides meals for thousands of at-risk individuals and helps train once-homeless adults in the culinary field.

Grant's Green Chile Posole

SERVES 6

1 tbsp olive oil
2 lb chicken tenders, or boneless, skinless breasts, cut into strips
1 medium yellow onion, chopped
3 cloves garlic, minced
4 (15-oz) cans hominy, drained
3 (32-oz) containers chicken broth
4 (2-oz) cans chopped green chiles
1 tsp dried oregano or 1 tbsp fresh oregano
Salt and ground black pepper, to taste
Flour tortillas, warmed and buttered, to serve

In a large pot over medium-high heat, warm oil. Add chicken and cook until it begins to brown, about 5 minutes. Add onion and garlic, and continue cooking until onions soften, about 2 minutes.

Add hominy, broth, chiles, and oregano and bring to a boil. Reduce heat and simmer for 30 to 40 minutes. Remove from heat, and season to taste with salt and pepper.

Ladle into bowls, and serve with tortillas.

My wife Claudia is from New Mexico, and she introduced me to southwestern cooking soon after our first date. As our love blossomed like a cactus rose in spring, she took me home to meet her folks. Her stepfather, Grant, who was born in Silver City, New Mexico, in 1908, cooked with a simplicity that astounded me. Over stories of seeing Pancho Villa ride through town, he prepared what has become one of my favorite all

time meals, Green Chile Posole (pas-o-lee). Posole is what southern folks call hominy, which is a big, fat corn kernel. I had never had it before, and it was so unfamiliar that I hesitated at first, but one slurp will sell you on this Southwestern standard for life. Grant and June eventually moved east to live with us until they passed. Ever since then, every time I make this dish, I wink at the sky in homage to my sweet father, Grant.

ERIC LANGE

Eric Lange is an actor who has appeared on *Lost*, *Victorious*, *CSI*, *The Bernie Mac Show*, *Without a Trace*, *The West Wing*, *Law and Order*, and *Modern Family*.

Chili

SERVES 10 TO 12

2 lb ground beef chuck
1 lb bulk Italian sausage
3 (15-oz) cans favorite beans for chili such as pinto, kidney, etc., drained
1 (15-oz) can beans in spicy sauce
2 (28-oz) cans diced tomatoes with juice
1 (6-oz) can tomato paste
1 large yellow onion, chopped
3 stalks celery, chopped
2 bell peppers, seeded and chopped
2 green chile peppers, seeded and chopped
1 tbsp bacon bits
4 cubes beef bouillon
½ c beer
¼ c chili powder
1 tbsp Worcestershire sauce
1 tbsp minced garlic
1 tbsp dried oregano
2 tsp ground cumin
2 tsp hot sauce, like Tabasco®
1 tsp dried basil
1 tsp salt
1 tsp ground black pepper
1 tsp cayenne powder
1 tsp paprika
1 tsp granulated sugar
1 (10.5-oz) bag corn chips, like Fritos®, to serve
1 (8-oz pkg) shredded Cheddar cheese, to serve

In a large, heavy-bottomed pot or Dutch oven, add ground beef and sausage, and cook over medium heat, stirring occasionally, until browned.

Stir in beans, tomatoes, tomato paste, onion, celery, peppers, and bacon bits. Cook, stirring occasionally, until heated through. Then, add remaining ingredients, stirring to combine. Bring to a boil, cover, and then reduce heat so mixture is at a constant simmer. Cook for 1½ hours, stirring frequently to make sure chili isn't sticking to the bottom of the pan.

Taste chili, adjusting seasoning accordingly. Remove from heat, and serve with corn chips and shredded cheese.

Being from Cincinnati, I have a natural fondness for all things "chili." Whenever I find myself back in Cincinnati, one of the first things my parents and I must do is sit down for some Cincinnati chili. There are many varieties out there, but I happen to be a "Skyline Chili" man, myself. Dining on the local cuisine I grew up with is a central part of bonding time when I come home. It reminds us of those treasured days gone by and it's become a tradition and a ritual during my visits home. But, as we move away from home, our friends become our extended family, and those families form their own traditions. One of my extended family members in Los Angeles makes this chili for Super Bowl parties, and I've grown quite fond of it. So, no . . . it's not like what I get at home back in Cincy, but it is pretty darn good eatin'! Enjoy!

This recipe was used by me during Chili Appreciation Society International competitions, and it was perfected over two years of competition. It took me to the world level competition three times, and although I didn't win, I was glad to compete. The chile powder listed in the recipe is available from Pendery's Spice Shop (penderys.com) in Dallas, Texas. It is not absolutely necessary to buy Pendery's— any good spice provider is ok, but do not rely on just one chile powder. Some chiles are for color, others for heat, and the rest are for taste.

This is a "three dump" method of cooking. Give your spices extra flavor by grinding them in a small coffee grinder or spice grinder before adding to the chili. Every day is different, taste as you cook, and add or subtract according to your taste. If you find the chili too spicy, do not add cayenne. To convert this into a home-style chili, add canned kidney beans, pinto beans, or any other extender to stretch this chili out to serve more people without losing the basic taste.

Gil Hovey

Gil Hovey resides in Stuart, FL and is retired from the U.S. Army. He is not a professional cook and cooks just for the enjoyment. He has competed in chili cook-offs in Texas, New Mexico, Arizona, and Mexico.

Competition Chili

SERVES 4 TO 6

FOR THE CHILI:
1 (14½-oz) can stewed tomatoes, drained
1 (4-oz) can chopped green chiles
1 tbsp olive oil
2½ to 3 lb top or bottom round beef, cut into ⅜-inch cubes, with all visible gristle and fat removed
2 (10.5-oz) cans chicken or beef broth (or use one of each)

FOR THE FIRST SPICE DUMP:
1½ tbsp onion powder
1 tsp garlic powder
1 tsp Original Chile Blend
1 tbsp Pecos Red Chile Powder
½ tsp ground white pepper

FOR THE SECOND SPICE DUMP:
½ tsp ground black pepper
½ tsp onion powder
½ tsp ground white pepper
½ tsp garlic powder
1 tbsp cumin
1 tbsp San Antonio Red Chile Powder
1 tbsp McCormick® Chili Powder
1 tbsp Fort Worth Light Chile Powder
½ tsp salt

FOR THE THIRD SPICE DUMP:
1 tbsp San Antonio Red Chile Powder
1 tbsp Fort Worth Light Chili Powder
2 tsp cumin
½ tsp onion powder
1 tsp brown sugar
½ tsp cayenne powder

In a blender, add tomatoes and green chiles. Purée into a sauce and reserve.

In a large, heavy-bottomed pot or Dutch oven, add oil and warm over medium-high heat. Add meat in batches, and cook, stirring occasionally, until evenly browned.

Meanwhile, whisk spices for each dump together in three separate bowls. Set aside.

When all the meat is browned, return it all to the pot, and add reserved tomato-green chile purée and the first spice dump. Reduce heat so the mixture is at a simmer. Cook chili, stirring frequently, for 1 hour, adding only enough broth to keep the mixture loose.

Add the second spice dump and simmer for 1 more hour, again adding broth as needed.

Then, add half of the third spice dump and cook for 30 minutes. Add the remaining spice mix, and simmer for another 30 minutes. Taste chili, adjusting seasonings, as needed. Serve.

Jim McGovern

Jim McGovern is a congressman from Massachusetts and has held the office since 1997.

Aunt Geraldine McGovern's Irish Stew

SERVES 6

2 tbsp olive oil
2 bay leaves
3 lb beef chuck, cubed
2 onions, chopped
2 tbsp flour
1 (12-oz) bottle Guinness beer
1½ to 2 c beef stock
Salt and ground black pepper, to taste
1 lb carrots, peeled and diced
1 lb parsnips, peeled and diced
¾ c dried prunes, finely chopped
1 small rutabaga, diced
1 tbsp chopped parsley, to garnish
Cornstarch, as needed

Preheat oven to 300°F.

Heat oil in large heavy pot or Dutch oven over medium-high. Add bay leaves and cook until they crisp and brown slightly, about 1 minute. Remove from pan.

Add meat, browning in batches if necessary, and set aside. Add onion to pot and cook until soft and translucent, about 3 minutes. Return beef to pan and sprinkle with flour. Cook until flour begins to brown slightly, about 1 minute. Add beer, beef broth, salt, and pepper, and bring to a boil.

Cover pot with lid and place in preheated oven for 1 hour. Add remaining ingredients and return pot to oven to cook for 1 more hour, or until vegetables are tender. Stir in parsley and season with salt and pepper. If broth seems thin, thicken with a few tablespoons of cornstarch dissolved in beef stock. Serve.

The stew tastes even better if made a day ahead of time.

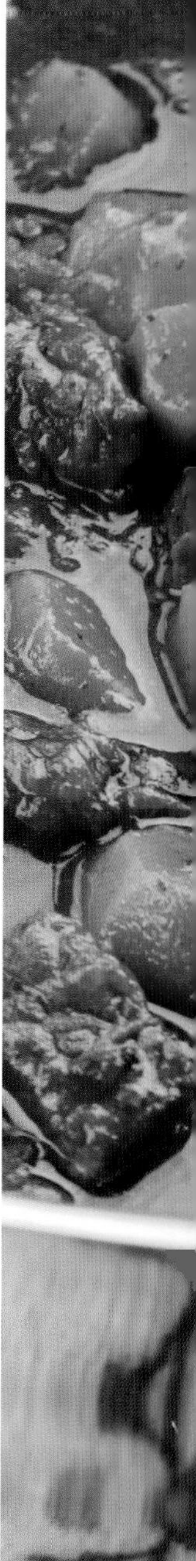

Phyllis Diller

Phyllis Diller is an actress, comedienne, and author. Diller received the American Comedy Award for Lifetime Achievement in 1992.

Chili

SERVES 4 TO 6

1 tbsp vegetable or canola oil
1 lb ground beef
1 medium onion, chopped
1 medium green bell pepper, chopped
10 cloves garlic, minced
1 tsp Lawry's® Seasoned Salt
½ tsp garlic salt
½ tsp onion salt
2 tsp chili powder
Tabasco,® to taste
1 (28-oz) can chopped tomatoes
2 (15-oz) cans kidney beans, like S & W Kidney Beans, undrained

In a large, heavy-bottomed pot, warm oil over medium-high heat. Add ground beef and cook, stirring occasionally, until beef is cooked through, about 10 minutes.

Add onion, bell pepper, and garlic, and cook until vegetables soften, about 3 minutes. Stir in seasonings and tomatoes, and reduce heat so mixture is at a simmer until chili begins to thicken slightly, about 20 minutes. Stir in kidney beans and their juice and simmer an additional 10 minutes. Taste to adjust seasonings, and serve.

S & W is a brand of seasoned canned beans. If you can't find them, substituting with any canned kidney beans will work just fine.

Spike Mendelsohn

Spike Mendelsohn was a contestant on the fourth season of *Top Chef* and also appeared on *Top Chef All Stars*. He also owns Good Stuff Eatery in Washington, D.C.

If anyone in this business could make money out of a stone, it was Uncle Denny. He had a club called the Blue Angel, which had a lab downstairs where he mixed bootleg liquor with legal liquor. He knew how to get the absolute most out of anything. He's been credited with watering down mustard, not giving lids or straws on cups, and telling people he's out of napkins when he had a whole supply stashed away. But his absolute best was whenever a cook was ready to pitch something, he'd look at it and say, "Put it in the chili!" It became a family joke, so how could we not name it after Uncle D?

Uncle D's Chili

SERVES 4

FOR THE CHILI:
2 lb ground beef
2 tbsp canola oil
1 c diced red onion
1 green bell pepper, seeded and diced
1 (16-oz) can kidney beans, drained, and rinsed
1 tbsp ground cumin
2 tbsp Hungarian paprika
1 tbsp chili powder
1 tbsp ground black pepper
1 (32-oz) can tomato sauce
1 c water
1 c chipotle barbecue sauce (recipe, below)
Salt, as needed
½ c cheddar cheese sauce (recipe, below)
½ c sour cream

FOR THE CHEDDAR CHEESE SAUCE:
2 c whole milk
¼ c unsalted butter
¼ c all-purpose flour
1 c grated sharp cheddar cheese
1½ tsp cayenne powder
Salt and ground black pepper

FOR CHIPOTLE BARBECUE SAUCE:
Half a (7-oz) can chipotle chiles in abodo sauce
2 c sweet, mild barbecue sauce
½ c ketchup
¼ c apple cider vinegar
1 tbsp molasses

Make the chili: Heat the beef in a large skillet over medium heat. Cook, stirring and breaking it up, until browned. Drain off the fat.

In large, heavy-bottomed pot over medium-low heat, heat the oil, and add onion and green pepper. Cook, stirring until softened until onion is translucent, about 10 minutes. Add the beans, cumin, paprika, chili powder, and black pepper. Increase the heat to medium and cook, stirring until the mixture is fragrant, about 4 minutes.

Add the browned beef into the pot, continue cooking and stirring until well mixed. Add the tomato sauce and water, and reduce the heat to medium-low. Cook, stirring occasionally, until the mixture thickens, about 1 hour.

Make the cheddar cheese sauce. Heat the milk in a large saucepan over medium heat until you see bubbles forming on top. Remove milk from heat. Meanwhile, melt the butter in another saucepan and stir in the flour to make a roux. Add the warm milk, whisking constantly, and continue cooking until the mixture thickens, about 5 minutes. Add the cheese, whisking constantly to combine. Season with the cayenne, salt, and pepper to taste. If desired, strain through a sieve to remove lumps before serving.

Make the chipotle barbecue sauce. Add the chipotles to a food processor or blender, and purée until smooth. Add the barbecue sauce, ketchup, vinegar, and molasses. Purée until smooth. Strain the mixture through a fine-mesh strainer to remove seeds.

To finish the chili, stir in the chipotle barbecue sauce and season with salt. Top each chili serving with 1 tablespoon of cheddar cheese sauce, and sour cream. Serve immediately.

STEVE SPITZ

Steve Spitz is a lifestyle TV personality and the host of *Living Better with Steve Spitz*.

New Mexican Green Chile & Pork Stew

SERVES 8

5 tbsp olive oil
2 large white onions, chopped
10 cloves garlic, minced
½ c flour
2 tsp ground cumin
1 tsp Mexican oregano
1 tsp ground sage
2½ lb pork tenderloin, cut into 1-inch pieces (pork butt or pork shoulder can be substituted)
6 lb roasted New Mexican Hatch Chiles, peeled, seeded, and coarsely chopped
5 c chicken stock, preferably homemade
1 (28-oz) can plum tomatoes, chopped, juice included
2 medium carrots, peeled and diced
2 lb white potatoes, peeled and diced
Salt and ground black pepper
Flour tortillas, warmed, as needed to serve

In a large, heavy-bottomed pot or Dutch oven, warm oil over medium-high heat. Add onions and garlic, and sauté until onions are translucent, about 3 minutes.

In a large, resealable bag, combine flour, cumin, oregano, and sage. Place pork in bag, seal it , and then shake vigorously to coat meat. Remove pork from bag and add to pot. Cook until lightly browned, about 5 minutes.

Add chiles to pot and cook, stirring frequently, for 10 minutes. Add chicken stock, tomatoes, and carrots. Reduce heat to low and cook, covered, for 2 hours, stirring occasionally. Add potatoes and cook, uncovered for 1 more hour. Season to taste with salt and pepper. Serve with warm flour tortillas.

For me, being asked to be part of a book like this magnifies the true essence of "the joy of cooking." Every time I step into my kitchen, a new opportunity arises—the ability to be creative in my own space in my own time, to experience the failures and successes, the hilarious and occasional train wreck of trial and error of cooking. I think we all share stories of good cooking gone bad—I know my family certainly does, from my sister's panflakes, also known as pancakes (FYI, if the box says to add both egg and water, I would suggest adding both egg and water. It seems pancakes become a new life form without eggs.) Other long-lasting memories include the time she caught my parents' kitchen on fire, my dad making gravy, and sitting on our kitchen countertop as a young boy watching my mom make homemade egg noodles.

Then there was the dreadful Sunday afternoon when I decided to make Tomato Basil soup. I had made this glorious soup so many times before but this Sunday I decided to purée it. I was such a young naive cook, unaware of so many potential disasters, and had somehow never learned the peril of filling a blender all the way to the top with piping hot liquid. It was as if an evil kitchen demon had planted a tomato bomb—spiked with an artillery of ingredients—set to detonate the very second I flipped on my blender. Seconds later, I stood covered in tomato basil hell! Oh, if I could turn back time—nothing in the room escaped its wrath. The entire kitchen, from the ceiling, walls, cabinets, appliances, sink, window, and backsplash never looked quite the same after that Sunday afternoon.

I love the multicultural America we live in today; it offers a robust melting pot of cultural and traditional flavors and introduces our palates to the possibilities of what we can do with food. Spending so much of my adult life in Santa Fe over the past twenty plus years has given me a brain trust of true Southwest-style cooking, unlike Tex-Mex and traditional Mexican. The recipe I'm sharing came from a gutsy, relentless determination to make the best Santa Fe Pork & Green Chile Stew ever! I make this every fall and winter for my friends and family, and it is my most requested recipe, hands-down.

The Ultimate
Swedish Meatballs . . . 79

Main Dishes: Beef

ADAM WEST

Adam West is the original Batman, on the television series *Batman* from 1966-1968 and in the film *Batman*.

Sawtooth Mountain Pot Roast

SERVES 6 TO 8

3 to 4 lb chuck roast of beef or elk
Salt and ground black pepper, to taste
1½ tbsp favorite dried herb, like oregano or rosemary
3 cloves garlic, cut into slivers
2 tbsp olive oil
1 large onion, chopped
2 stalks celery, chopped
4 to 5 slices green apple
1½ lb Yukon gold potatoes, quartered
3 medium carrots, peeled and sliced ½-inch thick
1 c red wine
1 c frozen green peas

Heat oven to 425°F. Season the meat with salt, pepper, and herbs. Use the tip of a knife to make several slits on the surface of the meat. Insert garlic into slits.

Heat olive oil in a large black iron skillet over medium heat. Add meat and brown the roast on all sides. Spread onion and celery around meat and place green apple slices on top of roast. Add 1 or 2 inches of hot water to the skillet. Cover the skillet tightly with foil and carefully place in oven. Cook for approximately 3 hours, checking periodically to make sure liquid does not evaporate.

Place potatoes in a large pot with just enough cold water to cover them. Bring to a boil, and then add carrots to the water. Cook for about 2 minutes until vegetables are partially cooked. Drain vegetables, reserving one cup of the vegetable cooking liquid.

Add the vegetables to the skillet, along with the reserved cooking liquid and wine. Cook roast for 1 more hour, and then stir in the peas. Continue cooking until peas are cooked through, about 5 minutes. Carefully remove skillet from oven. The meat should be fork-tender. Serve.

We've made a real effort to all have dinner together forever. It's a big plus for family unity and the kids' development, especially if the food is tasty and good. And it doesn't have to be Peking duck every night. My cast iron skillet Sawtooth Mountain Pot Roast is a real winner when it's my turn in the barrel. The meat cooks up super-tender and just pulls apart when carved. The aroma will be devastating.

The Amazing Kreskin

For six decades The Amazing Kreskin has become an integral part of pop culture, best known for his mind control, hypnotics, and magic shows.

The Barbecued Kreskin (Also Known as Burnt Toothpicks)

SERVES 2

Salt and ground black pepper, to taste
2 club steaks, ¼-inch thick, or Delmonico or New York strip steaks
4 slices bacon
5 tbsp butter
1 medium onion, chopped
1 medium green or red bell pepper, chopped
1 tbsp Worcestershire sauce, or to taste
2 tbsp chopped fresh basil
2 tbsp chopped fresh parsley

Preheat grill to medium-low heat.

Season each steak, and then wrap 2 slices of bacon around each steak and secure with a toothpick. Grill steaks to desired doneness—9 minutes on one side and 5 minutes on the other for medium rare.

Meanwhile, melt butter in medium sauté pan over medium-high heat. Add onion, bell pepper, Worcestershire sauce, basil, and parsley. Cook, stirring frequently, until vegetables are crisp-tender, 3 to 4 minutes.

Remove steaks from grill set aside to rest for 3 to 5 minutes. Place steaks on plates and top with the onion and pepper sauce. Serve immediately.

In recent years, a common inquiry has been made to me by people in the Western world. They ask, with the predictions I've made of the future and the increasing crime and the popularization by the so-called responsible media of degenerates, malcontents, and anti-social behaviorists, what do I suggest about protecting the quality of life in the culture surrounding our families today. I will respond by pointing out—Let's not talk about how many swimming classes your kids are taking or baseball games or social gatherings, just tell me one thing, and don't answer me publicly, because this will close the discussion. How many times a week do you, as a family, gather around the table and have meals together? I recommend serving with grilled baked potatoes and corn on the cob.

Dave Loebsack

Dave Loebsack is a congressman from Iowa. He has held the office since 2007.

Sloppy Joes

MAKES 4

1 lb ground beef
1 c water
¼ c chopped onion
2 tbsp Worcestershire sauce
¼ c ketchup
¼ c mustard
1 tsp garlic salt

In a large sauté pan over medium-high heat, add ground meat, and cook, stirring occasionally, until meat is browned, about 10 minutes. Remove from heat, and drain excess oil from ground meat.

Return to medium-high heat. Add water and stir in remaining ingredients. Simmer mixture for at least 1 hour, adding more water as needed to keep the mixture from drying out. Season to taste, and serve.

Thank you for allowing me the opportunity to contribute my recipe to the Made With Love: The Meals On Wheels Family Cookbook. *I am grateful for the work done by the organization across the nation. I have always been a supporter of Meals On Wheels and try to volunteer whenever I get the opportunity. Growing up in poverty in Iowa and being raised by my grandmother, I have seen first-hand what programs like it mean to many Iowans. I am grateful for the work of Meals On Wheels to my constituents.*

I have included my own recipe for Sloppy Joes. As a kid, I loved Sloppy Joes, and today I enjoy cooking it for my family. Every time my wife, Terry, and I prepare it, I am reminded of wonderful childhood memories. This is especially a great meal when paired with baked beans and chips.

FRED J. MORGANTHALL, II

Fred J. Morganthall is the president of Harris Teeter, a chain of supermarkets in the Southeast.

Almost-Homemade Beef Stroganoff

SERVES 4

1 tbsp butter or vegetable oil
1¼ lb boneless rib-eye or New York strip steak, thinly-sliced against the grain
½ cup diced sweet onion
1 box Hamburger Helper® Classic Stroganoff
⅓ c red wine
1 (4-oz) can chopped mushrooms plus liquid
1½ c milk
¾ c light sour cream

In a 12-inch sauté pan or skillet, warm butter or oil over medium-high heat. Add steak slices and onions, and sauté until the meat is browned and onions are translucent, about 5 minutes.

Stir in Hamburger Helper® sauce mix, wine, mushrooms, milk, and pasta from the package. Let mixture come to a boil, stirring occasionally. Cover, reduce heat to low, and simmer about 8 minutes.

Stir in sour cream and simmer, covered, an additional 4 minutes until sauce thickens. Remove from heat, uncover, and set aside for 2 minutes to allow sauce to continue to thicken. Serve.

Visit harristeeter.com for more dishes like this to prepare at home.

Gina Homolka

Gina Homolka is a chef and food blogger at SkinnyTaste.com, which was named one of *SHAPE* magazine's Best Healthy Eating Blogs 2011. Her recipes have been featured on sites including Glamour.com, Gourmet Live, The Kitchn, Finecooking.com, Fitness Magazine.

Skinny Italian Spinach Meatballs

SERVES 4 TO 6

FOR THE MEATBALLS:
2 slices whole-wheat sandwich bread
1 lb (93%) lean ground beef
10 oz frozen chopped spinach, thawed and drained
1 large egg
1 clove garlic, minced
2 tbsp fresh parsley
½ c grated Pecorino Romano cheese
Salt and ground black pepper, to taste
1 tbsp olive oil

FOR THE TOMATO SAUCE:
1 tsp olive oil
3 cloves smashed garlic
1 (28-oz) can crushed tomatoes, like my favorite, Tuttorosso
½ onion (not chopped)
Salt and ground black pepper, to taste

Make the meatballs: Wet bread with water, and then mash up with your hands. Add to large bowl and combine with beef, chopped spinach, egg, garlic, parsley, grated cheese, salt, and pepper. Mix all ingredients until thoroughly combined. Measure meat using a ¼ cup measuring cup, and divide in half, so each meatball is ⅛ cup. Roll into little meatballs, and reserve.

Meanwhile, make the sauce: In a large pot, add olive oil, and warm over medium heat. When hot, add smashed garlic. When garlic is golden brown, add tomatoes, onion, salt, and pepper. Cover sauce, and reduce heat to low.

While the sauce is cooking, heat a large nonstick frying pan on low heat and warm 1 tablespoon oil. When the oil is hot, add as many meatballs that will fit. Cook on low, turning often so that all sides are browned. Cook until the centers are cooked through.

When meatballs are cooked, transfer to a paper towel-lined plate to blot excess oil. Drop meatballs into sauce and continue cooking the remaining meatballs, repeating the process.

When all meatballs are in the sauce, simmer for an additional 15 to 20 minutes. Discard onion half, and serve.

I love sneaking vegetables into my recipe—it's the perfect way to get my picky kids to eat their veggies with an added bonus of making the meals I love lighter and healthier. Adding spinach to your meatballs adds volume and fiber, so you can eat the same amount of meatballs with fewer calories. But fear not, these meatballs are moist and flavorful with or without the sauce. They even got my very critical Italian husband's seal of approval.

I recommend making these meatballs on the small-side, so they hold together well. I can get 30 small meatballs out of this recipe, but only 25 will actually make it into the sauce because my husband and I can't stop eating them! Enjoy these delicious meatballs over your favorite pasta or on a crusty piece of Italian bread.

HEATHER AMARAL AND DIANE BRISSETTE

Heather Amaral is the executive director of Meals On Wheels of Rhode Island and Diane Brissette is the program's Home Delivered Program Director.

Rosie Thibeault's French-Canadian Dynamite

SERVES 12 TO 15

3 tbsp butter
1 large green pepper, diced, seeds removed
1 large red pepper, diced, seeds removed
2 medium onions, diced
2 large vine-ripened tomatoes, diced
1 c water
3 lb ground beef
2 to 3 (6-oz) cans tomato paste
1 tsp crushed red pepper flakes
1 tsp salt
1 tsp ground black pepper
½ tsp garlic powder
Torpedo rolls, also known as grinder rolls, as needed to serve

Melt butter in a large sauté pan over medium-high heat. Add peppers, onions, and tomatoes and cook until vegetables soften, about 3 minutes. Add water and cook until it's absorbed by the vegetables, about 2 minutes. Add ground beef and cook until evenly browned. Using a ladle, spoon off any grease that forms on the surface. (A little oil is fine, but you do not want a lot.)

Stir in the tomato paste, adding just enough paste to coat the meat. The consistency should not be too loose or mushy. Mix in seasonings, adjusting seasonings to taste. Remove from heat.

The dynamite will be stronger if left to mesh overnight, so keep this in mind when adding more seasonings. Refrigerate dynamite overnight to allow spices to blend.

To serve, reheat just before serving. Serve on torpedo rolls.

RoseAnna (Jodoin) Thibeault was making dynamites at Hamlet Lunch, which according to city directories of the time, was in operation at least from 1922 through 1925. No one knows where the idea for dynamites came from, but RoseAnna taught her daughter, Beatrice, how to cook them over the stove, and Beatrice showed her daughter and granddaughter. The dynamites remain a very popular menu item in local diners as well as for Meals On Wheels of Rhode Island recipients. The dynamite recipe can also be used as a topping on hot dogs.

Idie and Chris Hastings

Idie and Chris Hastings are chef and co-owners of the nationally celebrated Hot and Hot Fish Club in Birmingham, Alabama.

Few people knew that Idie's dad, Jim, had trouble digesting food due to Crohn's disease, an inflammatory disease of the gastrointestinal system. After all, Jim always looked forward to his next meal and delighted in the joys of eating while keeping his Crohn's disease in check. At home, he devoted an enormous amount of attention to reviewing his food intake. Since he was taking so many medications, he maintained as healthy a diet as possible with well-rounded meals containing a protein, starch, and green vegetable. He stayed away from sweets, except for the occasional pound cake, which became his favorite dessert as he grew older. Jim was diagnosed when Idie was just five years old, so she had a firsthand view of its progression and the effect certain foods had on him. He simply could not tolerate corn, which became a problem when he moved to the South to live with Idie late in his life. He found the temptation of Alabama sweet corn irresistible. At least once each summer he indulged in his corn "fix." Mostly, Idie remembers him eating small portions, many times a day, which consisted of the three round meals and smaller snacks in between.

Breakfast was a favorite of Jim's—he never missed it. There was always an egg, poached or scrambled, a piece of sausage or bacon, a side of fresh fruit and a cup of hot coffee. Jim often scolded Idie for skipping the morning meal—she was not a breakfast person.

It was fitting, upon his passing that Idie wanted to celebrate his life with family and food. Idie and Chris hosted a family-style dinner after his service—the way meals were served when she was growing up. Course after course appeared at the table while wine was poured, and guests shared stories of Jim and his wonderful life. When the Grilled New York Strip with Poached Egg and Rapini appeared at the table, Idie smiled as her eyes welled up with tears. There was that egg! Jim would have loved the dish—for breakfast!

Idie was surprised with a slideshow of old black-and-white photos of family get-togethers from her childhood. It was a time to laugh and reminisce. Zeb and Vincent, though young at the time, were present to witness and participate in this important rite of passage—of a life celebrated with food and family at a communal table. As the evening came to a close, Idie sat back quietly to observe the gathering and soak in the moment, knowing she could not have gotten through that day without her family's love and support. Since that day, in honor of Jim, the New York Strip with Poached Egg has been a mainstay on the Hot and Hot menu.

Grilled New York Strip with Poached Egg

SERVES 1

1 New York Strip Steak
1 Egg

Grill steak and serve with poached egg.

John Boozman

John Boozman is the United States senator from Arkansas. He served as a congressman from Arkansas for 10 years, from 2001 – 2011.

Barbecue Brisket of Beef

SERVES 8 TO 10

1 (4-lb) brisket, trimmed of fat
4 tbsp brown sugar, plus more for a sweeter sauce
1 medium onion, grated
1½ c ketchup
½ c freshly squeezed lemon juice
1 tsp prepared yellow mustard
Garlic salt, to taste
Celery salt, to taste

Preheat oven to 325°F. Line a 13- by 9-inch baking dish with enough aluminum foil on the ends and sides to seal securely around the meat. (This keeps sauce in place and makes clean-up easier.) Place brisket in center of the pan.

In a small bowl, stir brown sugar, onion, ketchup, lemon juice, and mustard together. Spoon sauce over brisket, and then sprinkle with salts.

Seal the foil securely around meat, and bake in preheated oven for 4 hours. Remove from oven, let cool, and place brisket in refrigerator overnight. (This makes it easier to slice.)

To serve, preheat oven to 350°F. Unwrap the foil and remove any solidified fat. Thinly slice the brisket and place back in the foil-lined pan with the sauce. Secure meat with foil again and place in preheated oven for 1 hour. Remove from oven, and serve.

This particular dish was chosen to be served when then Congressman Boozman entertained a few African Ambassadors. It was a hit with all.

John Schneider

John Schneider is an actor, best known for his role as Bo Duke in *The Dukes of Hazzard*. Schneider also starred in *Smallville* and has appeared in *Dr. Quinn, Medicine Woman*, *Touched by an Angel*, *JAG*, *Walker, Texas Ranger*, and *Diagnosis: Murder*.

Cap'n Crunch Meatloaf

SERVES 6 TO 8

Oil, as needed
1½ lb ground beef
¼ c chopped onion
¼ c quick-cooking oats
⅛ c cornmeal
1 c crushed Cap'n Crunch Cereal
1½ tsp salt
1 tbsp white sugar
1 egg, beaten
½ c tomato juice
½ c water
1 tbsp barbecue sauce
⅛ tsp liquid smoke flavoring, plus more as needed
1 tbsp distilled white vinegar
¼ c ketchup
1 tbsp brown sugar
2 tsp prepared yellow mustard

Preheat oven to 350°F and lightly grease a 9- by 5-inch loaf pan.

In a large bowl, combine beef, onion, oatmeal, cornmeal, Cap'n Crunch crumbs, salt, sugar, egg, tomato juice, water, barbecue sauce, liquid smoke, and vinegar. Mix together thoroughly and place in the prepared loaf pan.

In a separate small bowl, combine the ketchup, brown sugar, mustard, and 2 drops liquid smoke. Mix sauce thoroughly and spread evenly over the meatloaf.

Bake in preheated oven until meatloaf is fully cooked, approximately 1 hour. Let cool just slightly and serve.

My family loves meatloaf. And we love Cap'n Crunch cereal. So we combined our two favorite things and came up with this very special meatloaf recipe. Elly and I have always cherished our family meals together. As an actor, I can't always be home for dinner, but we try to have one meal together per day. We begin with a family prayer and talk about our kids' activities because I love hearing about my kids' lives. We've found that this family-time together keeps us connected to the kids, as well as keeping our kids grounded in our family values.

Kalle Bergman

Kalle Bergman is a food writer and the editor of the online food magazine, Honest Cooking. He is also a regular contributor to the *Los Angeles Times*, Huffington Post, and several Scandinavian food magazines.

Swedish Meatballs. The King Of Swedish Cuisine. The Classic of Classics. Titan Of Titans, if you will. This ultra classic has a very special place in the hearts of most Swedes. And why shouldn't it? It is after all a miniature version of the entire Swedish cuisine. It tastes like Sweden, and it has many of the classic ingredients that we see all across Scandinavian food culture like pickled cucumber, lingonberries, and cream sauce. Powerful and smooth at the same time. Sweet and sour. Simple but refined.

There are as many Swedish meatball recipes as there are Swedish mothers. All with their individual secrets and tweaks, and all claiming to be the original. Most use a bread and milk mixture to make the meatballs smoother, others mix pork and beef to make them lighter. Some season with everything from allspice to nutmeg. I use a little cream, dark beer, onions, and stock to make the meatballs slightly lighter, chunkier, and juicier. And they are mother-approved. Note: If you can't find Lingonberry jam (usually found in that Swedish furniture store), you can substitute red currant jelly. It's not the same, but it works.

The Ultimate Swedish Meatballs

SERVES 4

FOR THE PICKLED CUCUMBERS:
1 c vinegar
1 c water
1 tbsp salt
⅓ c sugar
1 to 2 cucumbers, finely sliced
1 bay leaf

FOR THE MASHED POTATOES:
2 lb potatoes
Salt and ground black pepper
½ c warm milk
3 tbsp butter

FOR THE MEATBALLS:
1 tbsp butter
1 onion, peeled and grated on a cheese grater
2 tbsp breadcrumbs
3 tbsp heavy cream
2 tbsp dark beer
2 tbsp beef stock
1⅓ lb ground beef
Salt and ground black pepper
Oil, as needed

FOR THE CREAM SAUCE:
½ c beef stock
1½ c heavy cream
1 tbsp butter
1 tsp cornstarch, mixed with a little cold water
Salt and ground white pepper
Pinch of sugar

FOR THE GARNISH:
Lingonberry or red currant jam, to serve
A few sprigs dill

Make the pickled cucumbers: In a large bowl, mix vinegar, water, salt, and sugar, whisking until sugar and salt is dissolved completely. Add cucumbers to mixture, making sure they are completely covered by the fluid. Add bay leaf, and put in the refrigerator for at least 1 hour.

Make the potatoes: Peel the potatoes and boil them in salted water until soft. Pass through a food mill into a large bowl to get the finest and smoothest mash. Add the butter and milk, slowly stirring into the potato mixture. Season with salt and add more butter if you want a creamier taste.

Make the meatballs: In a medium pan, melt butter over medium heat, and then gently fry the onion until golden brown. Remove from heat. In a bowl, mix breadcrumbs, heavy cream, beer, and stock in a bowl. Set aside for 5 minutes. Place the ground beef in a large bowl, add the browned onions and the breadcrumb mixture. Season with salt and pepper, and mix together well. Leave for 10 minutes.

Roll the meat into small balls with a diameter of roughly 1-inch. Fry them in batches with a sunflower oil, removing from pan when they are slightly crispy on the outside. Set aside while making the sauce.

Make the sauce: Deglaze the frying pan with a little water and add the stock. Bring to a boil over high heat, and reduce mixture half. Add cream, bring to a simmer, and thicken with butter and cornstarch. Let it simmer for 5 minutes. Taste and season with salt, sugar, and white pepper. Add the meatballs to the sauce, or serve them separately.

Serve meatballs and cream sauce with mashed potatoes, pickled cucumbers, and a side of jam. Garnish with dill, if desired.

Karen and Jamie Moyer

Jamie Moyer is a World Series champion MLB pitcher, He and his wife Karen Moyer founded the Moyer Foundation, which supports children dealing with trauma, distress, and loss.

Nana's Meatballs

MAKES 12 LARGE MEATBALLS

½ lb ground mild Italian sausage
¼ lb ground veal
¼ lb ground pork
1 lb lean ground beef
2 eggs, beaten
¼ c parsley, chopped
½ c grated Parmesan cheese, plus more to serve
1 c Italian seasoned breadcrumbs
Garlic salt, to taste
Dried oregano, to taste
2 (15½-oz) jars spaghetti sauce
1 lb pasta, cooked according to pkg directions

In a large bowl, mix ground meats, eggs, parsley, cheese breadcrumbs, garlic salt, and oregano together with your hands in a large bowl. Shape into baseball-sized balls.

In a large pot, add meatballs and cover with spaghetti sauce. Bring to a boil over high heat, and cover. Reduce heat to low and simmer for about 4 hours, stirring occasionally to make sure meatballs aren't sticking to the bottom of the pot. Remove from heat.

Add cooked pasta onto a serving platter and arrange meatballs on top. Pour sauce on top and sprinkle with Parmesan cheese.

A recipe from Nana Terry, who is a fantastic cook and really good at throwing ingredients together to make a really delicious meal. These meatballs are a family favorite, and a great recipe to share.

Sally Cameron

Sally Cameron is a chef, caterer and the author of the food blog, A Food Centric Life.

Barbecue-Glazed Meatloaf

SERVES 4

⅔ c of your favorite barbecue sauce
1 to 2 tbsp water, as needed
½ lb ground lean sirloin
½ lb ground turkey thigh
1⅓ c Japanese panko breadcrumbs
⅔ c finely diced onion
⅔ c peeled, finely diced Granny Smith apple
⅓ c ketchup
1 tbsp Dijon mustard
1 tbsp prepared horseradish
1½ tsp finely chopped fresh rosemary
1 tsp salt
½ tsp ground black pepper
1 egg
2 large garlic cloves, finely minced

Preheat oven to 350°F. Cover a rimmed baking sheet with heavy foil and spray with nonstick spray.

In a small bowl, add barbecue sauce and thin with a little water, stirring to get a glaze-like consistency. Set aside.

In a large bowl, mix the sirloin and turkey together with your hands, wearing disposable gloves if preferred. Add in remaining ingredients. Mix completely but don't over-handle it. If the mixture seems a little wet, add more panko.

Turn the mixture onto the prepared baking sheet and form into a compact, smooth loaf, like an oval loaf of bread. When the loaf is formed, pour a few tablespoons of barbecue glaze onto the loaf and spread over meatloaf with pastry brush. Reserve remaining glaze for later.

Place the meatloaf in the preheated oven and bake, brushing with glaze several times while baking. Cook meatloaf until done, registering 165°F on a meat thermometer, about 30 to 40 minutes.

Remove from oven and allow to cool a few minutes. Slice and drizzle with more glaze, if desired.

This is a healthier, modern take on the American classic comfort food with ground turkey, diced apple, and a barbecue glaze. Note that you can also make individual mini meatloaves by dividing the meat mixture into 4 small loaves. These will bake more quickly, so watch your timing. The classic side dishes to serve are green beans and mashed potatoes.

Moroccan Chicken or Tofu with Vegetables . . . 97

Main Dishes: Poultry

Oven-Baked Herbed Chicken

From *B. Smith Cooks Southern-Style* (Scribner, 2009)

SERVES 6

3 whole skinless, bone-in chicken breasts
2 c low-fat buttermilk
1 tbsp reduced-sodium soy sauce
½ tsp garlic powder
½ tsp onion powder
½ tsp poultry seasoning
¾ c plain breadcrumbs
½ tsp seasoned pepper blend, like Lawry's® Seasoned Pepper
½ tsp paprika
½ tsp dried thyme
Salt and ground black pepper, to taste

Cut each chicken breast in half, diagonally. Place chicken in a large bowl or resealable gallon-size plastic bag, and set aside.

In a medium bowl, add buttermilk, soy sauce, garlic powder, onion powder, and poultry seasoning, whisk together to combine. Pour buttermilk mixture over the chicken, cover or seal, and refrigerate. After 4 hours, remove the chicken from buttermilk marinade.

Preheat oven to 375°F. Prepare a baking sheet by coating with nonstick cooking spray. In large bowl, combine the breadcrumbs and seasonings. Roll the chicken pieces in the mixture, tossing to coat well.

Place the chicken on the prepared baking sheet bone-side down. Coat the chicken lightly with cooking spray. Bake in preheated oven until juices run clear when pierced at the bone with a sharp knife, about 30 to 35 minutes. Season with salt and pepper, and serve hot or at room temperature.

B. Smith

B. Smith is the owner of three successful B. Smith restaurants and has been recognized by *Elle Décor* as one of America's ten most outstanding non-professional chefs.

Historically a staple for Southern families, fried chicken is one of the most famous dishes in America—and also one of the first things I learned to cook in my mother's kitchen. Her recipe was very simple with no tricks or secret ingredients—easy to make and even easier to enjoy. These days, many people are watching what they eat and how it's prepared, including my husband, Dan Gasby, and myself. You'll find, as we did, that the Oven-Baked Herbed Chicken is just as satisfying as fried chicken, complete with a tangy flavor and the bonus of less fat. The tanginess is courtesy of buttermilk, which is lower in fat and calories than regular milk, because the fat from buttermilk has already been removed to make butter. This chicken is perfect for the holidays, allowing you to cut back on calories when feasting is unavoidable! Recipe from B. Smith Cooks Southern-Style *by Barbara Smith, published by Scribner, 2009.*

BECKY WAHLUND

Becky Wahlund is the director of Land O Lakes.

Cheesy Tomato Basil Chicken Breasts

SERVES 6

FOR THE SAUCE:
3 tbsp butter
⅓ c chopped onion
1 (6-oz) can tomato paste
2 medium tomatoes, cut into 1-inch cubes
1 tbsp dried basil
2 tsp minced garlic
½ tsp salt
¼ tsp ground black pepper
6 (6-oz) boneless, skinless chicken breasts

FOR THE TOPPING:
¾ c fresh breadcrumbs
¼ c chopped fresh parsley
2 tbsp butter, melted
8 (¾-oz) slices Provolone cheese, coarsely chopped

Preheat oven to 350°F. Add butter to a 13- by 9-inch baking dish and place in oven until melted, about 1 minute.

In a medium bowl, combine all remaining sauce ingredients, except the chicken; set aside.

Carefully remove baking dish from oven. Add chicken to the dish, using a fork to coat in butter. Spoon sauce evenly over chicken and bake in oven. Cook until chicken is cooked through, registering 165°F on a meat thermometer, about 30 to 40 minutes,

In a small bowl, combine breadcrumbs, parsley, and butter. Sprinkle chicken with cheese, and then breadcrumb mixture. Return to oven and bake chicken for another 5 to 10 minutes, until cheese is melted and breadcrumbs are browned. Serve.

Fresh tomatoes, basil, and Provolone cheese make chicken extra-special.

Chicken Tetrazzini

SERVES 8 TO 10

4 lb boneless chicken pieces
5 c chicken broth, divided
1 stick (½ c) butter
¼ c flour
1 c half and half
1 tbsp white wine
1 tsp salt
¼ tsp ground black pepper
1 (8-ounce) pkg spaghetti, cooked
⅓ c breadcrumbs
⅓ c Parmesan cheese

Preheat oven to 350°F.

In a medium pot, add chicken pieces and cover with 3 cups chicken broth. Bring to a boil over high heat. Cover with lid, reduce heat to medium-low, and simmer until chicken is cooked through, about 15 minutes. Transfer chicken pieces to a bowl, cool, and cut into pieces.

In a large sauté pan, melt butter over medium-high heat. Add flour, whisking to combine with butter and cooking for 2 minutes. Add remaining 2 cups broth, whisking again and cooking until thickened. Add half and half and cook 10 minutes. Stir in wine, salt, and pepper. Add the chicken pieces into the sauce.

Meanwhile, arrange cooked spaghetti in a 9- by 13-inch buttered dish. Pour chicken mixture over the spaghetti.

In a small bowl, mix breadcrumbs and cheese. Sprinkle evenly over top of casserole. Bake for 25 minutes. Remove from oven, and serve.

Cathy Green Burns

Cathy Green Burns is the President of Food Lion supermarkets.

A recipe that has been in our family for more than 50 years, my claim to fame growing up was that this casserole was the only dish my mom made that I could eat more of than my dad could! Now, this is a favorite meal of my husband and my two daughters. We enjoy making and eating the casserole together. Alexis loves testing the spaghetti and Maia has a ball adding the finishing touch of breadcrumbs and cheese. This recipe makes a great casserole to give to a new family moving into the neighborhood, a mother just coming home with a new baby, a friend who has just been released from the hospital, or to take along to a reunion. To do this, just assemble the dish, cover with foil, and pass on with the directions to bake at 350°F for 30 minutes.

Florence Henderson

Florence Henderson is an actress, best known for her role as Carol Brady in *The Brady Bunch*. Henderson has been named one of the 100 Greatest TV Icons by TV Land and *Entertainment Weekly*. She also hosts *The Florence Henderson Show* on RLTV.

When I was raising my children, we all ate together, and we all ate the same thing together! My how things have changed; families today face so many more schedule issues and dietary challenges. I hope you enjoy my recipe; Mrs. Brady wants your family to eat it together—and don't leave the table until your plate is clean.

To toast the pine nuts, place in a skillet over medium heat, and cook, stirring frequently, until they're golden. Nuts can also be toasted in a 350°F oven, stirred occasionally, for 10 to 15 minutes. Recipe from Florence Henderson's Short-Cut Cooking, *published by William Morrow, 1998.*

Chicken Piccata with Pine Nuts & Capers

From *Florence Henderson's Short-Cut Cooking* (William Morrow, 1998)

SERVES 4

½ c milk
2 large eggs
½ c all-purpose flour
Salt and ground black pepper
4 (6-oz) boneless, skinless chicken breasts, pounded into thin pieces
½ stick (¼ c) unsalted butter, divided
¼ c vegetable oil
⅓ c lemon juice
⅓ c white wine (or apple juice, white grape juice, or chicken broth)
2 cloves garlic, minced
2 tbsp capers, rinsed and drained
¼ c minced fresh parsley
½ lb spaghetti, cooked al dente, to serve
¼ c toasted pine nuts, to garnish

In a small bowl, add milk and eggs, and slightly beat together. In another dish, add flour, salt, and pepper.

Dip the chicken pieces into the milk mixture and then into the flour mixture, coating each piece well. Shake off excess flour, and reserve on a plate.

Meanwhile, in a large, shallow skillet, warm 2 tablespoons butter and all the vegetable oil over medium-high heat. Add the coated chicken pieces to the hot skillet and cook until the chicken is no longer pink on the inside, about 4 minutes on each side. Remove the chicken from the pan and drain on paper towels. Reserve and keep warm.

Reduce the heat to medium-low and add the remaining 2 tablespoons butter to the pan drippings. Stir in the lemon juice, wine, and garlic. Stirring constantly, cook for 2 to 3 minutes. Add capers and parsley, stirring and cooking for about 1 minute.

To serve, place a serving of pasta on each plate and top each with a chicken breast. Spoon sauce over each serving and sprinkle with pine nuts. Serve immediately.

Fran Drescher

Fran Drescher is an actress, best known for her role on *The Nanny*. Also an author and healthcare advocate, Drescher founded the Cancer Schmancer Movement, an organization to help diagnose women's cancers early, in 2007.

Fran's House Chicken

SERVES 4 TO 6

1 tbsp extra-virgin olive oil
4 organic boneless, skinless chicken breasts, cut into thin cutlets
2 tbsp Dijon mustard
1 tbsp basil pesto

Preheat broiler.

Coat a small baking dish evenly with the oil. Add chicken to baking dish and schmear mustard evenly on both sides of chicken. (The mustard is where all the flavor comes from, so spread liberally.) Add pesto, schmearing it over all the chicken.

Place chicken in broiler until chicken is cooked through and fragrant, about 10 minutes. Remove chicken from oven and let rest for 5 minutes before serving.

We gals from Queens know how to make discount clothes look couture and easy recipes to taste gourmet. Like Sara Lee, nobody doesn't like Fran's House Chicken—even my dog, Esther, is a fan. Amounts are to taste. If you like it saucy, add a smidge more mustard or pesto. Remember chicken continues to cook after you take it out of the oven. You can always cook it more, but you can't uncook it. Plus, nobody likes dry, overcooked chicken; not even Esther! Serve this warm, at room temperature, or cold. This chicken is great on a salad, in a sandwich, cut into pasta, served with a side of vegetables, or as a quick protein snack. My fridge is never without Fran's House Chicken. Enjoy, doll!

Linda Gray

Linda Gray is a television actress, best known for her role as Sue Ellen Ewing on *Dallas*.

Roast Chicken

SERVES 4 TO 6

1 (5- to 6-lb) whole chicken, rinsed and patted dry
3 tbsp olive oil, divided
Salt and ground black pepper, to taste
1 lemon, quartered
3 garlic cloves, peeled and crushed
1 small onion, halved
4 sprigs fresh rosemary

Preheat the oven to 450°F.

Rub the chicken with 1 tablespoon of oil and sprinkle generously with salt and pepper. Stuff the chicken's cavity with the lemon, garlic, onion and rosemary.

Heat remaining 2 tablespoons oil in a large, cast iron skillet over medium-high heat. Add the chicken and cook, rotating frequently, until evenly browned on all sides. Remove from heat, and position chicken breast-side-up in the pan.

Transfer skillet into the preheated oven. Roast the chicken for 45 minutes to 1 hour.

Reduce the oven's temperature to 375°F until a meat thermometer inserted in the thickest part of the thigh reaches 180°F, about 20 to 30 minutes.

This is a chicken recipe that never fails with the kids (and grandsons) loving it! I start with Grandma Betty's cast iron skillet—which is always a good thing to have on hand. I stuff the chicken and sear it on all sides, using a long-handled wooden spoon to turn the bird in the pan. Some of the stuffing will fall out, but just shove it back in! The high temperature gets the skin crispy. Serve the chicken with lots of veggies, a big salad and . . . there you go! Enjoy!

Shane and Melissa Victorino

Shane Victorino is a MLB outfielder for the Philadelphia Phillies. Shane and his wife Melissa, run the Shane Victorino Foundation, which helps provide opportunities for underserved children.

Chicken Katsu

SERVES 4

FOR THE CHICKEN:
4 skinless, boneless chicken breast halves, pounded to ½-inch thickness or 1½ lb chicken tenders
Salt and ground black pepper, to taste
¼ c all-purpose flour
1 large egg, beaten
1 c panko breadcrumbs
Vegetable oil, for frying
Garlic powder, to taste

FOR THE DIPPING SAUCE:
½ c Worcestershire sauce
¼ c ketchup
2 tbsp soy sauce
Salt and ground black pepper, to taste

Season the chicken breasts on both sides with salt and pepper.

Place the flour, egg, and panko breadcrumbs into 3 separate shallow dishes. Coat the seasoned chicken breasts first in flour, shaking off any excess. Dip them into the egg, and then press chicken into the panko until well-coated on both sides.

In a large skillet, fill with ¼-inch of oil and warm over medium-high heat. Carefully place breaded chicken in hot oil and cook until golden brown, about 3 or 4 minutes per side.

To make the dipping sauce, add all ingredients into a small bowl. Season to taste. Serve sauce with breaded chicken.

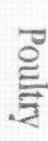

Meals On Wheels does great work, and we are proud to do our small part in helping to advance their mission. Because we run our own non-profit, the Shane Victorino Foundation, we appreciate the need for collaboration to make a difference in the lives of those we serve.

Tessie Santiago

Tessie Santiago is an actress, who has appeared on *Queen of Swords*, *Kitchen Confidential*, *Curb Your Enthusiasm*, and *One on One*.

Turkey Picadillo

SERVES 6

1 tsp olive oil
1 lb ground dark-meat turkey
½ medium onion, chopped
½ Cubanelle green pepper
4 cloves garlic, peeled and crushed
¼ c olives
¼ c raisins
¼ tsp dried oregano
¼ tsp cumin
½ c tomato sauce
¼ c white wine

Warm oil in large sauté pan over medium-high heat. Add turkey and cook until brown, about 7 minutes. Add onion, pepper, and garlic, and cook, stirring occasionally, until translucent, about 3 minutes.

Add remaining ingredients, stir to combine, and cook for 4 to 5 minutes. Reduce heat to low, and simmer an additional 10 minutes, until picadillo thickens slightly. Remove from heat and rest for 10 minutes before serving.

I love a Cuban Christmas Eve dinner, or as we would call it, Noche Buena. We roast an entire pig in a makeshift oven in our backyards that we call a Caja China. Our side dishes consist of rice, black beans, plantains and yuca. For dessert, you can always count on a variety of choices to spike your insulin level. One of the most traditional, turon, a delicious end-of-the-night treat that is followed by a perfect cafecito to help with digestion. Another traditional Cuban dish is picadillo, and here is my healthier version made with turkey. You can serve this with rice or even put it in pasta. It's delicious!

Salmon Baked
in Parchment . . . 110

Main Dishes: Seafood

AL ROKER

Al Roker is a national television weatherman and personality, best known for his work on NBC's *Today*.

New Orleans-Style Barbecued Shrimp

From *Al Roker's Big Bad Book of Barbecue* (Scribner, 2007)

SERVES 8

4 lb fresh or frozen (21 to 25 count per pound) large or extra-large shrimp, in the shell
5 tbsp chili powder, divided
1 tbsp plus 2 tsp salt, divided
2 sticks (1 c) unsalted butter
2 medium onions, peeled and finely chopped
6 cloves garlic, minced
1 c ketchup
½ c extra-virgin olive oil
5 tbsp light brown sugar
¼ c Worcestershire sauce
1 lemon, sliced
3 tbsp freshly squeezed lemon juice (from 1 lemon)
3 bay leaves
2 tsp dried oregano
2 tsp dried thyme
1 tsp cayenne powder
Several dashes Louisiana-style hot sauce

First, prepare the shrimp. You can buy large, frozen tiger shrimp that have been deveined but are still in the shell. If you use these, thaw them according to the package directions. If using fresh shrimp, ask the person at the fish counter to devein them for you in the shell. This can also be done by yourself, using kitchen shears. Cut the shell along the vein and pull the vein out with your fingers. Or, you can just skip the deveining process. The vein won't hurt you.

In a small bowl, combine 3 tablespoons of the chili powder and 1 tablespoon of the salt. Rub the shrimp with this mixture, making sure you rub some into the open cut where the shrimp has been deveined (if it has) to season the shrimp inside the shell. Place the seasoned shrimp in a shallow, non-reactive pan, cover with plastic wrap, and refrigerate while you make the sauce.

In a saucepan over medium-high heat, melt the butter. Add the onion and garlic, and cook for 3 to 5 minutes, until softened but not browned. Add the ketchup, oil, brown sugar,

Worcestershire sauce, lemon slices, lemon juice, bay leaves, oregano, thyme, cayenne, and hot sauce, as well as the remaining 2 tablespoons chili powder and 2 teaspoons salt. Stir to mix. Reduce the heat so the mixture is at a simmer, and cook, covered, stirring occasionally, for about 20 minutes, or until thick. Remove from the heat, uncover, and cool to room temperature. Remove and discard the lemon slices and bay leaves.

Pour 1½ cups of the sauce over the seasoned shrimp. Toss to coat well. Cover and refrigerate the shrimp for 1 to 2 hours, also refrigerate the remaining sauce separately for dipping.

Prepare a charcoal fire or preheat a gas grill for direct grilling over high heat.

While the grill is heating, reheat the remaining sauce in a small, covered saucepan over very low heat—it will only take a few minutes. Watch the sauce carefully, so it doesn't burn.

Remove the shrimp from the pan and discard the marinade. Grill the shrimp for 2 to 3 minutes per side, until the shells are orangey-pink in color. To test for doneness, take a shrimp off the grill, remove the shell, and cut the shrimp in half: the flesh should be white and firm throughout.

Serve shrimp with the warm sauce for dipping, and a large bowl for the shells.

In New Orleans, barbecued shrimp is actually cooked on the stovetop. This is an adaption for the grill. Cover the picnic table with brown paper, get a stack of paper napkins, and go to town. Don't blame me if that loudmouth Emeril Lagasse shows up. I'm kidding. Really. BAM! Recipe from Al Roker's Big Bad Book of Barbecue, *published by Scribner, 2007.*

Debbie Case

Debbie Case is the President and CEO of Meals On Wheels Greater San Diego.

Wild Rice & Barley with Roasted Tuna Steak

SERVES 8

1 lb fresh tuna steaks
Salt and ground black pepper, to taste
¾ c extra-virgin olive oil
⅓ c freshly squeezed lemon juice
1½ tsp Dijon mustard
1 large garlic clove, minced
¼ tsp ground white pepper, to taste
3 c cooked rice
3 c cooked barley
1 c chopped red bell pepper
1 c chopped green bell pepper
5 scallions, chopped
2½ tbsp slivered almonds

Preheat oven to 400°F.

Place tuna on a foil-lined baking sheet. Season with salt and pepper, and cook until just cooked through, 12 to 15 minutes. Remove from oven and reserve.

In a small container with a lid, add olive oil, lemon juice, mustard, garlic, and white pepper. Fit tightly with the lid and shake vigorously until dressing is well-mixed. Set aside.

In a large bowl, combine rice, barley, bell peppers, and scallions. Add dressing and toss until evenly coated. Season to taste with salt and pepper, and divide salad evenly among 8 plates. Thinly slice reserved tuna, and distribute among plates (2 ounces of tuna for each serving). Sprinkle with almonds and serve.

Meals On Wheels Greater San Diego is a recipient of freshly-caught unwanted fish from sport fishermen being distributed by a local charity, "Fish. Food. Feel Good." These nutritious fish are cleaned, filleted, and donated to us and several other charities who serve it to Americans in need, whether that need originates from being elderly, homeless, jobless, a military veteran, or something else. Our Meals On Wheels "University" interns from San Diego State University developed healthy meals that are diabetic-friendly, plus low in sodium and fat for our seniors, like this recipe.

Mark Dayton

Mark Dayton is the governor of Minnesota, having previously served as the United States senator from Minnesota for six years.

Salmon Baked in Parchment

SERVES 2

2 (6-oz) salmon fillets
2 tsp extra-virgin olive oil
2 shallots, thinly-sliced
1 clove garlic, minced
1 sprig fresh rosemary, halved
1 sprig fresh oregano, halved
A few fresh chives
A few sprigs fresh thyme
2 lemon slices
3 tbsp white wine
Salt and ground black pepper
2 sprigs parsley, to garnish (optional)

Preheat oven to 400°F.

Place 2 (12-inch) parchment squares on a baking sheet, using foil if you don't have parchment paper. Add the salmon fillet to the center of the parchment square. Drizzle each fillet with olive oil, and then top with evenly divided shallots, garlic, herbs, and lemon slices. Pour white wine over each fillet and season with salt and pepper. Wrap parchment over fish, folding to seal it tightly (You want the salmon to steam inside the packet.).

Place baking sheet into the oven, and cook fish 8 to 10 minutes, depending on thickness of fish.

Remove fillets from parchment packets and transfer to plates. Discard herbs, leaving the shallots, lemon and garlic remaining. Pour any remaining juices from the parchment over fish. Garnish with parsley, if desired.

Baked Salmon in Parchment is a favorite dish of Governor Dayton's. The executive chef at the Governor's Residence, Micah Pace, perfected this recipe while working in Talkeetna, Alaska.

Patti LaBelle

Patti LaBelle is a Grammy-winning singer, whose hit song "Lady Marmalade" was inducted into the Grammy Hall of Fame in 2003. LaBelle is also a successful actress, having appeared on film, television, and on Broadway.

Baja Fish Tacos

SERVES 8

¼ c mayonnaise
¼ c sour cream
Mild hot sauce, like Ms Patti's Cilantro Lime Hot Sauce, to taste
2 c shredded cabbage
1 c diced tomato
½ c diced red onion
Salt and ground black pepper, to taste
¾ c cornmeal
½ tsp garlic powder
½ tsp onion powder
¼ tsp cayenne powder
½ c olive oil
1 lb tilapia fish fillets
8 tortillas, warmed

To make the slaw, in a large bowl, add mayonnaise, sour cream, and hot sauce, to taste, mixing together to combine. Add cabbage, tomatoes, and onion, tossing until evenly coated. Season to taste with salt and pepper. Reserve.

In another large bowl, combine cornmeal, spices, and salt.

Add oil to a large skillet, and warm over medium-high heat. Dredge fish in cornmeal mixture and add to hot oil. Cook until golden brown and crispy, about 2 to 3 minutes per side. Transfer cooked fish to a paper towel-lined plate to drain excess oil.

To serve, place ¼ cup of slaw in the center of each tortilla. Divide fish evenly among tortillas and add more hot sauce to taste. Fold tortillas in half and serve!

My Baja Fish Tacos are a quick and easy meal that the whole family will enjoy. They are perfect for any occasion, especially summertime barbecues.

Mrs. Kostyra's Potato Pierogi . . . 119

Main Dishes: Vegetable

Helen Mirren

Helen Mirren is an Academy Award-winning actress, known for her roles in *The Queen*, *Elizabeth I*, *Prime Suspect*, *Calendar Girls*, *Door to Door*, and *Gosford Park*. She is also an accomplished stage actress, performing on the West End and Broadway.

Mironoff Piroshki

MAKES 6 TO 8 PIES

3 tbsp butter
½ c water or chicken stock
1 medium white cabbage, thinly sliced
2 leeks, thinly sliced
1 medium onion, chopped
2 refrigerated pie crusts
3 hard-boiled eggs, chopped
3 tbsp chopped parsley
Milk, for brushing the crust

Preheat oven to 350°F.

Combine butter and water or stock in a large sauté pan and warm over medium-low heat. Add vegetables and cook, stirring occasionally, until vegetables soften, about 10 minutes. The cabbage should still have a bite. Remove from heat, and set aside to cool.

On a floured surface, roll pie crusts out to a ¼-inch thickness. Cut into 6 (½-inch) circles and set aside.

Once the vegetables have cooled, drain, and place in a large bowl. Add eggs and parsley, and then season to taste. Stir to combine.

Divide vegetable filling evenly between the pastry circles, placing filling in center of each circle. Brush edges of crust with milk, then pinch edges together to seal pies together.

Place pies on lightly greased baking sheet. Lightly brush the tops of the pies with milk. Bake in preheated oven until golden brown, about 20 to 25 minutes.

Our father was born in Russia, on the family estate called Kuryanova. The upheaval of the Russian Revolution and World War I left him and his parents living in London. In later years, his father came to live with us. Grandpa loved nothing better than to sit and tell his grandchildren tales of his life in Russia. We think that this version of piroshki *must be from a recipe he told our mother; she adapted it and these cabbage pies have been firm family favorites ever since. We know they are not authentic* piroshki*; but they are an original Mironoff Piroshki!*

Martha Stewart

A prolific author and successful businesswoman, Martha Stewart is the founder, president, and CEO of Martha Stewart Living Omnimedia, where she is the host of her syndicated talk show *Martha* and publisher of *Martha Stewart Living* magazine.

My mother, Big Martha as she was known in the family, loved to cook and bake. She had an army to cook for, and she did it with ease and reliability. My father, siblings, and I were the daily beneficiaries of variety, fresh ingredients, multiple dishes, and delicious homemade desserts. There was no such thing as fast food in our lives, unless you could call the paper-thin minute steaks we all loved on white bread with butter, salt, and pepper fast food. We rarely, if ever, opened cans—no soft drinks, no junk food—but we had lots of homemade cookies and cakes and pies, to keep our sweet teeth happy and fulfilled. Mom wasn't a health freak, and always believed in a balanced diet with milk, butter, meat, fish, lots of vegetables, and some sweets.

I think all six children grew up unfussy and experimental about food because Mom was so adventurous herself, trying new ingredients and encouraged by our father's love of the exotic. We were never bored, never complacent, and we always looked forward to meals prepared in the kitchen and served to the entire family at one sitting.

Mom had an extensive collection of wonderful recipes, but my favorite was and still is pierogi, little boiled dumplings concocted from a round of tender, plain dough. The half-moon shape is formed around a savory filling, such as a soft pillow of potato, or occasionally a sweet one, such as an apricot or halved plum.

If my mother's recipes are better in my mind than others I have tried, it is because she was uncompromising in her fastidious search for perfect ingredients. She insisted, for example, that potatoes be yellow-fleshed and rich, and that the butter and sour cream come from a local dairy, not the supermarket.

She had an expert touch in making soft, tender, malleable dough. Other recipes for dough do not have both milk and sour cream, and most do not call for rolling it as thin. I use a cookie or biscuit cutter for the rounds, but I never saw Mom use anything except the floured rim of a specific glass tumbler with perfectly straight sides. She cut her circles very, very close together, so as not to waste a centimeter of dough, which she rolled out only once. I never saw her reuse the scraps. She said they would not make a perfect dumpling.

Before she passed away several years ago, I worked very closely by my mother's side, writing down her recipes, so we would all have them forever. I am happy to share her pierogi recipe with you.

Mrs. Kostyra's Potato Pierogi

MAKES ABOUT 5 DOZEN

1 large egg, lightly whisked
2 tbsp sour cream
1 c whole milk
1 c water
5 c all-purpose flour, plus more for surface and dusting
Yellow cornmeal, for dusting
5 lb (about 12 medium) Yukon gold potatoes, peeled and quartered
Salt and ground black pepper
8 oz cream cheese, at room temperature
4 tbsp melted unsalted butter
2 sticks (1 c) unsalted butter

In a large bowl, whisk together egg and sour cream. Add in milk and water, whisking to combine. Stir in flour, 1 cup at a time.

Turn out dough onto a floured surface. (Dough will be loose and sticky.) Using a bench scraper, turn and fold dough to knead, dusting with flour as needed, until elastic and no longer sticky, 8 to 10 minutes. (Dough will come together as you knead it. Be careful not to add too much flour, since it will toughen the dough.) Cover with an inverted bowl; let rest for 1 hour.

Meanwhile, make the filling: Place potatoes in a large pot, and cover with cold water. Season with salt. Bring to a boil, and cook until potatoes are fork-tender, 8 to 9 minutes. Drain potatoes, and then pass through a ricer. Stir in cream cheese and melted butter; season to taste with salt and pepper.

Divide dough into 4 equal pieces. Line a rimmed baking sheet with a clean linen towel, and dust generously with cornmeal to prevent sticking. Roll out 1 piece of dough on a lightly floured surface into a ⅛-inch-thick round (keep other pieces covered).

Cut out circles very close together, using a 3-inch cutter or glass. Cover with plastic wrap to prevent dough from drying. Repeat with remaining dough.

Form filling into 1½-inch ovals (about 1 tablespoon plus 2 teaspoons each). Place filling in the center of each dough circle. Holding 1 circle in your hand, fold dough over filling. Pinch edges, forming a well-sealed crescent. Transfer to cornmeal-dusted towel, and loosely cover with plastic wrap. Repeat with remaining dough circles and filling.

Meanwhile, bring a large pot of salted water to a boil. Working in batches, transfer pierogi to boiling water. They will sink to the bottom and then rise. Once they have risen, cook through, about 2 minutes more. Remove from water, and reserve.

To make the brown butter, melt the 2 sticks of butter in a small saucepan over medium heat, swirling occasionally, until dark golden brown, 8 to 10 minutes. Coat a platter with half the brown butter. Transfer pierogi to platter using a slotted spoon. Drizzle tops with remaining butter, and season with salt. Serve.

Qingxin Cai

Qingxin Cai is the staff accountant for the Meals On Wheels Association of America.

Moo Shu Egg

SERVES 4

3 tbsp olive oil, divided
2 scallions, thinly chopped
3 eggs, beaten
1 cucumber, thinly chopped
1 c dried, shredded wood ear mushrooms, rehydrated in boiling water
2 oz vermicelli rice noodles
½ tsp salt
¼ c water

In a wok or large skillet, heat 1 tablespoon olive oil over medium-high heat. Add in scallions and beaten eggs and cook, without stirring, until firm. Flip the eggs over and cook for an additional minute to firm the other side. Set egg pancake aside to cool and then slice into thin strips.

Heat the remaining 2 tablespoons oil in a wok or large skillet over medium heat. Stir in cucumber and rehydrated mushrooms, and cook for 2 minutes. Add vermicelli, salt and water; continue cooking until the vermicelli softens, about 2 minutes.

Stir in sliced egg pancake and cook, stirring until slightly thickened and hot, about 4 minutes. Serve.

It is always amazing to me how one bite can conjure a vivid memory. We all have these taste memories; specific flavors that, when we experience them, remind us of a time, a place or a person. I have many of these taste-induced moments, but one of my favorites is the memory I associate with vermicelli and wood ear mushrooms. Three years ago, I decided to pursue a higher degree overseas. My parents were worried about me being not accustomed to the diet, so they started teaching me how to prepare the home-style Chinese dishes before I left, and this Moo Shu Egg is the one I learned first. Now, three-odd years later, I still feel the same way each time perfect vermicelli and wood ear mushrooms hit my tongue. That love of summer, family, giving, cherishing, and sharing has been preserved in me by this recipe.

Tom Costello

Tom Costello is a journalist and correspondent for NBC News, and his reports have been aired on *Today*, *NBC Nightly News*, *MSNBC*, and *CNBC*.

Belgian Endives with Ham & Cheese

SERVES 4

3 tbsp butter, divided
8 Belgian endives, removed of stem and core
Pinch of nutmeg
Salt and ground black pepper, to taste
Pinch of sugar
1 c water
8 ham slices
2 tbsp flour
½ c milk
Juice of 1 lemon
1 c grated Gruyere cheese
Bread or mashed potatoes, to serve (optional)

Preheat oven to 400°F.

In a large sauté pan over medium heat, melt 1 tablespoon butter and add endives. Sprinkle with nutmeg, salt, pepper, and sugar. Add water, cover, and simmer endives until fork tender, 8 to 10 minutes.

Transfer endives into a bowl, reserving the cooking liquid. When endives are cool, lightly squeeze to get rid of any excess liquid. Wrap each endive with a slice of ham and place in a baking dish.

In a small pot over medium heat, melt remaining 2 tablespoons of butter. Add flour and cook, whisking constantly for 1 minute. Gradually whisk in milk, reserved endive cooking liquid, and lemon juice. Cook until sauce thickens slightly, about 2 minutes.

Pour the sauce over the endives in the baking dish and sprinkle with cheese.

Place in the preheated oven, and bake 20 minutes. Then, preheat broiler, and place dish under broiler until cheese browns, 2 to 5 minutes, depending on the strength of your broiler. Serve immediately.

This is a recipe from my Belgian wife, Astrid. A national dish of Belgium is Belgian endives with ham and cheese. While Astrid became an American in 2008, her home of Belgium is still very important to her. She only speaks Flemish to our two daughters, she enjoys cooking meals from home, and we travel to Brussels at least once a year. So here is Astrid's dish and a taste of Belgium.

Beef Enchiladas . . . 128

Casseroles

James Clyburn

James Clyburn is a congressman for the state of South Carolina. He has held the office since 1993.

Hamburger Casserole

SERVES 6 TO 8

1 lb lean ground beef
1 c cooked rice
1 (10.7-oz) can cream of chicken soup
1 (10.7-oz) can cream of mushroom soup, or 1 (10.7-oz) can golden mushroom condensed soup
1¼ c water
½ tsp salt
Pinch of ground black pepper
¼ c chopped green pepper
¼ c chopped onion
½ c grated cheddar cheese

Preheat oven to 350°F.

In a large sauté pan over medium-high heat, add ground beef and cook until browned, about 10 minutes. Remove from heat, and drain excess oil from ground meat.

Add degreased ground meat to a large bowl, and stir in remaining ingredients, except cheese.

Pour mixture into a 2½-quart casserole dish. Place in preheated oven and cook 35 minutes. Sprinkle casserole with cheese and cook for another 10 minutes. Remove from oven, and serve.

This is one of the congressman's favorite dishes to eat when he comes in from a late-night flight. This is a fairly inexpensive and easy-to-make dish that can be served with a green salad and crusty bread.

Jeanette Herbert

Jeanette Herbert is the First Lady of Utah. Her husband, Governor Gary Herbert, has held the office since 2009. She is known as "First Lady Jessie."

Beef Enchiladas

SERVES 4 TO 6

2 lb ground beef
½ medium onion, chopped
1 tsp oil
8 corn tortillas
1 (10-oz) can mild Old El Paso® Enchilada Sauce
1 (10.7-oz) can condensed tomato soup
2 c grated mild cheddar cheese
Sour cream, chopped tomatoes, chopped avocados, and shredded lettuce, to serve

Preheat oven to 350°F.

In a large sauté pan over medium-high heat, add ground beef and onion, cooking until the beef is browned, about 10 minutes. Set aside.

In another sauté pan, warm oil over medium heat, and lightly cook tortillas, turning once, just until heated through and pliable.

In a medium bowl, mix enchilada sauce and tomato soup together. Dip each tortilla in the enchilada mixture. Fill each tortilla with ground beef mixture, and then drizzle with sauce. Sprinkle with cheese then roll each tortilla and place in a 9- by 13-inch baking dish. Pour remaining sauce onto enchiladas and top with remaining cheese.

Bake in preheated oven 30 to 35 minutes, until heated through and cheese is melted. Serve with accompaniments.

The hearty beef enchilada recipe is a favorite of Utah Governor Gary Herbert. The entire Herbert Family, six children and spouses, plus 13 grandchildren, gather often to enjoy each other's company and devour this delicious dish.

Baked Spaghetti

From *Lady & Sons Savannah County Cookbook* (Random House, 2008)

SERVES 4

2 c canned diced tomatoes
2 c tomato sauce
1 c water
½ c diced onion
½ c diced green bell pepper
2 cloves garlic, chopped
¼ c chopped fresh parsley
1½ tsp Italian herb blend, like Paula Deen's Sweet Italian Herb Blend
1½ tsp seasoned salt, like Paula Deen Seasoned Salt
1½ tsp sugar
2 small bay leaves
1½ lb ground beef
½ (16-oz) pkg angel hair pasta, cooked according to pkg directions
1 c grated cheddar cheese
1 c Monterey Jack cheese

In a stockpot, combine the tomatoes, tomato sauce, water, onions, peppers, garlic, parsley, spices, sugar, and bay leaves. Bring to a boil over high heat, and then reduce the heat and let simmer, covered, for 1 hour.

Crumble the ground beef in a large skillet. Cook over medium-high heat until fully cooked, with no pink color remaining. Drain the fat from the meat, and then add the ground beef to the stockpot. Simmer for 20 more minutes.

Preheat oven to 350°F.

Cover the bottom of a 13- by 9- by 2-inch pan with sauce. Add a layer of pasta and then a little less than half of each cheese (saving a little cheese to top at the end); repeat the layers, ending with the sauce.

Bake in the preheated oven for 30 minutes. Top the casserole with the remaining cheese, return it to the oven, and continue to cook until the cheese is melted and bubbly, about 5 more minutes. Cut into squares before serving.

Paula Deen

Paula Deen is a chef, author, restaurateur, and TV host. Deen won an Emmy award for her Food Network show, *Paula's Home Cooking*, in 2007, and she is also the publisher of *Cooking with Paula Deen* magazine.

Ever since I opened The Lady & Sons restaurant in Savannah, Georgia, with the help of my two sons, Jamie and Bobby, our baked spaghetti has been a crowd favorite. We still serve baked spaghetti on The Lady & Sons buffet, and this recipe was featured in my very first cookbook. My baked spaghetti is affordable, easy-to-make comfort food that will never let you down. Fodor's *travel guide even called it, "The best baked spaghetti in the South."*

I'm so glad to be part of this cookbook. We live in the richest country in the world, and nobody should go to bed hungry at night, especially seniors. These people spent their whole lives caring for others, and we cannot forget about them when they need us most. That's why I love Meals On Wheels programs, because they work to make sure that seniors never go hungry.

Sam Donaldson

Sam Donaldson is a broadcast reporter who has served as the news anchor for ABC News since 1967.

Enchiladas

SERVES 2 TO 4

1 (15-oz) can of red chile sauce or enchilada sauce
Canola or vegetable oil, for frying tortillas
4 corn tortillas
1 medium yellow onion, chopped
2 c shredded cheddar cheese
2 tbsp chopped cilantro
Sour cream, refried beans, and chopped green chiles, to serve

In a medium skillet, add chile sauce and warm over low heat.

Then, warm oil over medium heat in a medium-sized skillet. Using tongs, carefully dip one tortilla in the hot oil just until it softens. (Do not overcook or it will fall apart.) Dip the softened tortilla into the warm chile sauce and place it flat into a glass baking dish. Sprinkle tortilla with a quarter of the cheese and a quarter of the onion.

Repeat with remaining tortillas, frying and dipping them in enchilada sauce, stacking on the previous tortilla and topping with cheese and onion. Sprinkle cilantro over the top tortilla.

Spoon remaining sauce over stacked tortillas and bake in preheated oven 10 to 12 minutes. Remove from oven and serve immediately with accompaniments.

I'm from the Southwest where enchiladas are the favorite food (or at least mine). If you really want the authentic recipe that's served on a linoleum table cover in an adobe hole-in-the-wall café, you will have to make your own tortillas, whip up a batch of chile sauce from scratch, use yellow onions direct from the field, and freshly-packaged Longhorn cheddar cheese. But who has the time or expertise to do that? So, using store-bought ingredients, here is the recipe for flat enchiladas. (The rolled kind are for outlanders.)

Jennifer Huffman

Born and raised in Johnson City, Tennessee, far from her Greek heritage, Jennifer has always had a passion for food and cooking. She loves cooking and entertaining for her friends and family, including her daughter, Lainey.

Champion Chicken Casserole

SERVES 6 TO 8

2½ to 3 lb boneless, skinless chicken breasts
Salt and ground black pepper
2 tsp olive oil
1 medium onion, chopped
1 (10.75-oz) can cream of chicken soup
1 (16-oz) container sour cream
1 (12-oz) box cheese crackers, like Cheez-It® crackers, crushed
1 stick (½ c) butter, melted
1 (16-oz) bag extra-wide egg noodles, cooked according to pkg directions

Preheat oven to 350°F.

Place chicken breasts in large pot and add just enough water to cover by 1 inch. Bring to a boil over high heat. Cover, reduce heat so liquid is simmering, and simmer until chicken is cooked through, 20 to 25 minutes. Remove chicken from pot and set aside to cool.

When chicken has cooled, use a fork to shred into pieces. Season with salt and pepper, and layer on bottom of a large casserole dish.

Heat olive oil in a medium sauté pan over medium-high heat. Add onion and cook, stirring occasionally, until soft, about 3 minutes. Spread onion evenly over chicken.

In a medium bowl, stir soup and sour cream together. Pour over chicken, spreading evenly. Sprinkle crushed crackers over soup mixture and drizzle casserole with melted butter.

Bake in preheated oven until golden brown and bubbly, about 45 minutes. Serve casserole over egg noodles.

I wanted to share this recipe that my mother has made for me and my siblings and now our children. This is such a good meal for a family gathering as everyone always comes back for seconds. I love to make this for my family and friends, and they all ask for the recipe.

Greetings from the great state of Alabama from Alabama's fifty-third governor. I was born on February 3, 1943, in Columbiana, Alabama, and grew up in the Joiner Town subdivision, where my mother used to make homemade peach and apple pies. She would pick peaches and apples, and slice them to lie on a hot tin roof. Then, she would cover them in cheesecloth until they dried. She would store the slices in jars to be used during the winter when she made fried peach and apple pies. There isn't an exact recipe for her pies because she cooked to taste, and no one can make the pies as well as she did.

If my mother was still alive and able to bring over one of her famous pies, there would be no comparison as to what my favorite dish is. However, as a close second, Poppy Seed Chicken Casserole will have to do.

Robert Bentley

Robert Bentley is the governor of Alabama, previously serving in the Alabama House of Representatives.

Poppy Seed Chicken Casserole

SERVES 6 TO 8

2 sleeves of buttery crackers, like Ritz,® crushed, divided
1 stick (½ c) butter, cut into small pieces, divided
4 chicken breasts, cooked and cut into bite-size pieces
1 (10.7-oz) can cream of mushroom soup
1 (10.7-oz) can cream of chicken soup
1 (8-oz) container sour cream
¾ c chicken broth
2 tbsp poppy seeds
2 c cooked white rice, to serve

Preheat oven to 350°F.

Line the bottom of a 13- by 9-inch baking dish with half the crushed crackers. Dot the crackers with half the butter. Spread chicken pieces evenly over the crackers.

In a medium bowl, stir soups, sour cream and broth together. Pour over chicken and top with remaining crushed crackers and butter. Sprinkle casserole with poppy seeds.

Cover casserole with foil and bake in preheated oven for 25 minutes. Remove foil and continue cooking for an additional 5 minutes, until crackers are golden-brown. Serve with rice.

Spinach and Goat Cheese Gnocchi with
Sun-Dried Tomatoes, Pine Nuts, & Lemon . . . 146

Pastas and Rice Dishes

Dawn Wells

Dawn Wells is an actress best known for her role as Mary-Ann on *Gilligan's Island*.

Weenie Linguine

From *Mary-Ann's Gilligan's Island Cookbook* (Rutledge Hill Press, 1993)

SERVES 4 TO 6

1 lb Italian sausage, removed from casings
1 stick (½ c) butter
1 clove garlic, chopped
1 medium onion, chopped
½ tsp dried oregano
1 tsp dried basil
½ tsp dried tarragon
¼ c fresh parsley
2 c sliced mushrooms
8 oz linguine, cooked al dente and kept warm
1 c heavy cream
Parmesan cheese, to taste
Salt and ground black pepper, to taste

In a large skillet over medium-high heat, sauté crumbled sausage, stirring until cooked through, about 10 minutes. Remove sausage from pan and set aside.

Return pan to heat and add butter, cooking until melted. Add the garlic, onion, herbs, and mushrooms and cook, stirring occasionally, until vegetables soften, 3 to 5 minutes. Return sausage to the pan and cook until heated through.

Toss in the cooked linguine, heavy cream, and Parmesan. Season to taste with salt and pepper. Mix well, tossing until linguine and sausage are evenly coated with sauce. Serve.

My mom was a fabulous cook and so were both my grandmothers. Even though my Grandmother Wells wasn't Italian, she made fabulous homemade raviolis from scratch.

One Christmas, my mother, Grandmother Wells and I spent three days hand-making raviolis from scratch; all the herbs and spices and meats for the stuffing, rolling the dough very thin, cutting it in strips, stuffing and sealing each ravioli by hand in my grandmother's kitchen in Reno.

Then, on Christmas day we served a huge platter of the homemade raviolis, and I believe the total count was 250! It took us three days, not including the days of shopping and setting a beautiful table. When we sat down to a wonderful meal, my father ate them all in 20 minutes! We have laughed about it ever since. And now that both my mother and grandmother are gone, I haven't made homemade raviolis since.

Enjoy my Weenie Linguini recipe which is my mother's—and has nothing to do with hot dogs—as my contribution to say thank you for the wonderful work Meals On Wheels does for seniors.

With my cousin, Liz's, engagement to an Italian guy from Puglia came an entire new Italian wing to our already extended Jewish family. Although his mother, Mamma Rosa, speaks not a word of English, and I not a word of Italian, we managed to use the language of food to communicate. She taught me the family sweet potato gnocchi recipe which I promptly mastered and then personalized to make it my own favorite dish. It also satisfies my ego that it's the favorite dish for my family and friends too!

Doug Liman

Doug Liman is a director and producer, best known for his work on such films as *Swingers*, *The Bourne Identity*, and *Mr. & Mrs. Smith*.

Momma Rosa's Gnocchi

SERVES 6

FOR THE GNOCCHI:
1 lb sweet potatoes, peeled and quartered
1 egg
1 tsp salt
3 to 4 c flour, plus more for dusting

FOR THE SAUCE:
3 tbsp vegetable oil
2 c peeled and julienned parsnips
10 to 15 fresh sage leaves
2 tbsp olive oil
4 c sliced mushrooms of choice, like shiitake or button
3 cloves garlic
2 tbsp white wine
Freshly grated Parmesan cheese, to taste

Make the gnocchi: Place potatoes in a large pot. Add 2 quarts of water and bring to a boil over high heat, cooking until potatoes are fork-tender, about 40 to 45 minutes.

Drain potatoes, patting dry with paper towels, and place in a large bowl. Mash potatoes with a fork until smooth. Add the egg and salt, and then gradually stir in the flour until it is the consistency of a moist dough (It can be lifted out of bowl as one sticky mass.). Place dough on a lightly-floured surface and knead gently, sprinkling lightly with flour to prevent sticking.

Divide dough into 4 equal pieces. Roll one piece into a rope about 1-inch thick. (Cover the remaining pieces of dough with a moist cloth to keep from drying out.) Place one rope on a lightly-floured cutting board and cut it into 1-inch pieces. Press each piece gently with the tines of a fork.

Bring 3 quarts of salted water to a boil. Add the gnocchi in batches to keep from overcrowding, and cook until they float to the surface, about 3 minutes.

Use a slotted spoon to remove gnocchi from water and place them immediately into the warm sauce.

Make the sauce: Heat vegetable oil in small sauté pan over medium-high heat. Add julienned parsnips and cook until lightly brown, about 2 minutes. Use a slotted spoon to remove parsnips from oil and set on paper towels to drain. Add sage leaves to hot oil and cook until crispy, but still green, about 1 minute. Remove from oil and set on paper towels to drain.

Heat olive oil in a large sauté pan (large enough to hold the gnocchi) over medium-high heat. Add mushrooms and garlic, and cook until they begin to brown, about 2 minutes. Reduce heat to medium low and add half the fried sage leaves and the wine. Add cooked gnocchi and stir until coated with sauce. Add reserved parsnips and the remaining fried sage leaves. Sprinkle with Parmesan and serve.

Joe Regalbuto

Joe Regalbuto is an actor and director, best known for his work on *Murphy Brown*, *Missing*, *The Sword and the Sorcerer*, and *The Golden Girls*.

Linguini al a Pesto

SERVES 4

1 lb linguine
1 bunch fresh basil, about 2 c basil leaves
4 cloves garlic
½ c extra-virgin olive oil
½ c freshly grated Parmesan cheese

Cook pasta in a large pot of heavily-salted boiling water. Stir the pasta occasionally to prevent it from sticking together. Cook until al dente, about 9 minutes.

While the pasta cooks, combine basil, garlic and olive oil in food processor, and purée until a thick paste forms. Add cheese, purée just a couple seconds to combine, and place pesto in a large serving bowl.

Drain pasta and add to bowl with pesto. Use tongs to toss until pasta is evenly coated. Serve.

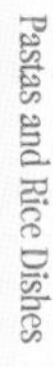

My father, who was born in Italy, taught me how to make this when I was ten. Though it was not a traditional Sicilian recipe and pesto is used more traditionally in the northern cities like Genoa and Portofino, it didn't matter! The flavor stayed with me, and so did the name, as I named my corporation, Pesto Productions. The more basil you use, the greener and more flavorful the pesto will be. Some people use pine nuts, but my father never made it that way. I too never use pine nuts, but feel free to add them to this recipe.

Spinach & Goat Cheese Gnocchi with Sun-Dried Tomatoes, Pine Nuts, & Lemon

From *Simple Italian Food* (Clarkson Potter, 1998)

SERVES 4

Kosher salt, as needed
1 lb fresh spinach, well-washed, stems removed
1 lb ricotta cheese, or Coach Farm fresh goat cheese
2¼ c all-purpose flour
2 extra-large eggs
½ tsp freshly grated nutmeg
¼ c freshly grated pecorino cheese, plus more for sprinkling
1 stick (½ c) unsalted butter
½ c sliced sun-dried tomatoes
3 tbsp pine nuts
Juice and zest of 1 lemon

Bring about 6 quarts of water to a boil and add about 2 tablespoons salt.

Make the gnocchi: In a medium saucepan, steam the spinach over medium-high heat in just the water that clings to the leaves. When just wilted, drain well. Chop very fine, then wrap in a dish towel and squeeze to remove as much moisture as possible.

In a large bowl, stir the ricotta cheese until softened. Add the spinach, then the flour, eggs, 1 teaspoon salt, nutmeg, and pecorino, and stir to form into a firm ball. Divide into 4 balls and knead on a cutting board until firm and slightly dry. Roll each ball into 1-inch pieces and roll down a fork to create traditional gnocchi shape. Continue until all the dough has been shaped.

Place all the gnocchi into the boiling water and stir once. Cook until all float to the top, 6 to7 minutes.

While the gnocchi cook, combine the butter, sun-dried tomatoes, and pine nuts in a 12- to 14-inch sauté pan. Cook over medium heat until the butter is lightly browned, then add the lemon juice and zest, and remove from the heat.

Drain the gnocchi gently, add to the pan with the sauce mixture, and return to medium heat. Toss to coat and serve immediately. Sprinkle with additional cheese at the table.

Mario Batali

Chef and restaurateur Mario Batali has written nine cookbooks, hosted and starred in cooking shows on The Food Network and PBS, and founded the Mario Batali Foundation, which helps feed children.

These gnocchi have the velvet texture of my grandma's recipe, but also use Coach Farm's wonderful goat cheese. I love that this recipe combines generations of tradition on the Batali side with the delicious cheese that my wife's family produced for years in upstate New York. To me, this dish is reminiscent of the simplicity of dishes in Italy and of memorable family meals here in the States. Recipe from Simple Italian Food *by Mario Batali, published by Clarkson Potter, 1998.*

Paul Sanchez

Paul Sanchez is a guitarist and singer-songwriter whose songs have been performed by artists such as Hootie and the Blowfish, Susan Cowsill, Kevin Griffin, John Boutte, and The Eli Young Band.

Pop's Pasta

SERVES 4 TO 6 (OR ONE VERY LARGE MAN, 6'5" 245 POUNDS AND HIS TWO GROWING SONS)

Salt, as needed
1 lb pasta
1 lb ground turkey breast
½ tsp garlic salt
1 c shredded fat-free mozzarella
½ c I Can't Believe It's Not Butter!®

Bring a large pot of heavily-salted water to a boil over medium-high heat. Add pasta and cook until al dente. Drain pasta and place it back in the pot. Cover and set aside.

Lightly coat a large sauté pan with nonstick cooking spray and heat over medium heat. Add turkey and cook, using a spatula to break up the turkey meat into small pieces. Season turkey with garlic salt and cook until turkey is browned and cooked through.

Add half the cooked turkey, half the cheese and half the butter substitute to the pasta and toss until well-mixed. Add the remaining turkey, cheese, and butter substitute. Toss and serve.

I'm a divorced father who grew tired of take-out every time my sons were over, so I came up with the one and only meal my boys and I could make together and not burn down the house! My boys prefer rigatoni, but you can substitute your favorite pasta. After making this pasta, I like to put on a great DVD. My boys prefer Ace Ventura 2: When Nature Calls.

Rosa DeLauro

Rosa DeLauro is the U.S. congresswoman from the state of Connecticut.

Pasta DeLauro

SERVES 6 TO 8

Salt and ground black pepper, to taste
⅓ c olive oil
1¼ lb onions, thinly sliced (about 3 large onions)
1 lb linguine
8 large eggs
1¼ c finely-grated Parmigiano-Reggiano
¾ c minced parsley

Bring a large pot of salted water to a boil.

Heat olive oil in a large, heavy-bottomed pan and add onions. Cook, stirring occasionally, until onions are brown and very soft , approximately 30 minutes.

While the onions cook, add the linguine to the salted water and cook according to package instructions.

In a large bowl, beat eggs and stir in the grated cheese and parsley. Season with salt and pepper.

When linguine is cooked, use tongs to transfer noodles from water directly to pan with the sautéed onions. Stir until well-mixed. Add the eggs to the linguine and onion mixture, stirring well with a large fork as the eggs cook. Season to taste and serve.

My grandmother is from the Amalfi coast of Italy, and my grandfather was a pastry chef and owned a bakery in my hometown of New Haven, Connecticut. They passed on their knowledge and love of cooking to their children, who in turn passed it on to my generation. Cooking was a major part of our lives, and our families ate together every Sunday. To me, cooking is therapy. This is a dish that I love to serve my friends and family, and it is always popular. I hope you enjoy it as much as we do.

Stephanie Gallo

Stephanie Gallo is the Vice President of Marketing at E&J Gallo Winery in Modesto, Calif.

Linguine with Tomatoes & Basil

SERVES 4 TO 6

4 ripe large tomatoes, cut into ½-inch cubes
½ lb Brie cheese, rind removed, torn into irregular pieces
1 c fresh basil leaves, cut into strips
3 garlic cloves, minced
½ c plus 1 tbsp good-quality olive oil, divided
2½ tsp salt, divided
Freshly ground pepper, as needed
1½ lb linguine
Freshly grated good-quality Parmesan cheese (optional)

In a large serving bowl, combine tomatoes, Brie, basil, garlic, ½ cup olive oil, ½ teaspoon salt, and pepper. Prepare at least 2 hours before serving and set aside, covered, at room temperature.

When ready to serve, bring 6 quarts water to a boil in a large pot. Add 1 tablespoon olive oil and remaining 2 teaspoons salt. Add the linguine and boil until tender but still firm, 8 to 10 minutes.

Drain pasta and immediately toss with the reserved tomato sauce. Serve at once, passing the peppermill, and grated Parmesan cheese if you like.

Our grandmother, Amelia Franzia Gallo, had two passions: cooking and her family. Amelia believed the best meals included fresh ingredients from the garden, prepared so you could taste all their robust flavor. We used to gather vegetables with her from the garden behind her house, then enjoy the aromas as she cooked family meals in the kitchen. Today, we gather vegetables with our own children, but our minds always turn back to those sunlit afternoons with Amelia, watching her two passions join so perfectly into one. We hope you enjoy this special recipe which is easy to prepare and a great way to showcase summer vegetables. Also, it pairs deliciously with Gallo Family Vineyards' Pinot Grigio.

Al Franken

Al Franken is the junior United States senator from Minnesota also known for his previous time in film and television, most notably on *Saturday Night Live*.

Wild Rice & Turkey Hot Dish

SERVES 12 TO 14

1 lb wild rice, like Mahnomen wild rice
1 stick (½ cup) butter
3 medium yellow onions, sliced
4 stalks celery, thinly sliced
10 cloves garlic, sliced
2 lb white button mushrooms, sliced
Salt and ground black pepper, to taste
6 c roasted turkey, pulled from the bone
Turkey gravy or drippings

Place rice in a colander and rinse under cold water. Drain and place rice in a large, heavy-bottomed pot. Cover with 3 inches of water and boil, uncovered, for 20 to 25 minutes. (If you're using Mahnomen wild rice, it will cook more quickly than the paddy variety.)

Melt butter in a large sauté pan over medium-high heat. Add onions, celery, and garlic, and cook, stirring occasionally, until vegetables just begin to soften, about 2 minutes. Add mushrooms and cook until they begin to brown, about 2 minutes more, (Be careful not to overcook the vegetables. They should still have a bite to them.)

Drain cooked rice and add it to the pan with the vegetables. Stir in pulled turkey and any roasting juices. Season to taste with salt and pepper, and serve.

My mom was a great cook, and to this day I still miss some of the dishes she made. One of my all-time favorites was her wild rice stuffing. As a kid growing up in St. Louis Park, Minnesota, my family went to a lot of potlucks. Every time we went to one, my Mom would bring her stuffing, and, of course, it was always a big hit. And it just wasn't Thanksgiving in the Franken house without her stuffing on the table. My wild rice and turkey hot dish is my own variation on her original recipe. Now my kids insist that I make it for Thanksgiving, and I'm more than happy to do so because it reminds me of my mom and her great cooking.

Derek Lee

Derek Lee is a food writer and creator of The Best Food Blog Ever, which has been featured in *Saveur* magazine.

Fried Rice with Egg

SERVES 4 TO 6

2 tbsp vegetable oil, divided
3 large eggs, lightly beaten
2 tbsp minced garlic
2 tbsp minced ginger
4 c cold cooked rice
1 c diced meat or shellfish, cooked (optional)
4 tbsp soy sauce, or to taste
½ c thinly sliced scallion greens (3 to 4 scallions)
1 tbsp Asian sesame oil

In a wok or large frying pan, warm 1 tablespoon vegetable oil over high heat until shimmering. Add the egg and tip the pan to coat the bottom evenly. Cook for 1 to 2 minutes, flip with a spatula, and then continue cooking for another minute, or until the egg is completely cooked. Use the spatula to roll the egg into a loose bundle, then remove the egg from the pan and set aside.

Add the remaining 1 tablespoon of oil to the pan and heat until shimmering. Add the garlic and ginger and sauté, stirring frequently, until the mixture is fragrant and the garlic begins to color.

Add the rice and use a spatula to break up any large chunks. Stir to coat the rice evenly with oil, adding more oil if the mixture seems dry. Add meat or shellfish, if using, to the pan and stir to distribute it evenly throughout the rice. When the rice is heated throughout, add the soy sauce and stir until the rice is evenly coated.

Return the egg to the pan, using your spatula to break it up into bite-size pieces. Remove from heat, then add scallions, and sesame oil, stirring to incorporate. Serve.

Growing up Chinese, fried rice made an appearance on the dinner table at least once a week. At the time, I didn't even realize that one of the reasons for its heavy rotation was just how convenient and economical it is to prepare—the ingredients are inexpensive and readily available, it transforms leftover rice into a quick meal, and it's a great way to make use of small amounts of leftover meat that would otherwise not be enough to feed more than one person. As a kid, I remember my mother making a simplified version of this dish for lunch using only eggs and oil, and it was just as delicious. While a wok is convenient for this recipe, any large frying pan will do just as well.

Joe Garagiola

Joe Garagiola was a catcher in the MLB from 1946-1954. He went on to become a popular sports announcer and television host.

Risotto

SERVES 12

10 c chicken broth
½ c margarine
3 tbsp canola oil
8 slices bacon, chopped
2 large onions, diced
2 (20-oz) container chicken livers, chopped
½ tsp salt
6 c uncooked rice
Saffron, to taste
1 (15-oz) can sliced mushrooms
¾ c grated Parmesan cheese

In a large, heavy-bottomed pot, bring broth to a boil.

In a large skillet, combine margarine, oil, and bacon and cook until bacon begins to brown. Add onion and cook until browned, about 5 minutes. Stir in chicken livers and salt, and cook until livers are evenly browned. Add rice and cook for another 2 minutes.

Add rice mixture to boiling broth, stirring well, and simmer until rice is cooked, about 25 minutes. Stir in saffron, mushrooms, and cheese. Risotto should be creamy, so add additional broth if rice is dry. Serve.

I wish hitting a baseball would be as easy as it is for me to name my favorite dish. When my mother or father would make risotto, it was like World Series time at our house. Risotto made Sunday the special day of the week for me. In fact, risotto would make any day special for me. When risotto was served on Sunday there was always enough for lunch on Monday. I was never a speedy runner as a baseball player and had my speed described on a scouting report as deceptively slower than he looks, but I know my speed was always much better on the Monday after Sunday risotto because I ran all the way home from school to be sure I was not the last one to sit down.

My favorite risotto always had chicken liver mixed in with the rice. I've eaten it with mushrooms, pieces of white chicken, bacon, the list goes on. I believe I would like it if they added diced hockey pucks. I know you won't forget the fresh grated Parmesan cheese for the finishing touch.

I'm lucky that my wife makes Hall of Fame risotto. I can also add that when we have a special day to celebrate, our daughter-in-law joins in with her recipe and we have an extra-great dinner.

Maya Angelou

Maya Angelou is a *New York Times* bestselling author and poet. Angelou has been awarded the Presidential Medal of Freedom and the National Medal of Arts and her work has received nominations for a Pulitzer Prize, Grammy Award, Tony Award, and National Book Award.

Jollof Rice

SERVES 8 TO 10

3 c long-grain rice, divided
¼ c plus 2 tbsp peanut oil, divided
1 (10.5-oz) can beef consommé
1 tsp salt
3 c water, plus more as needed
1½ c chopped onion
3 c diced, cooked ham
1 (28-oz) can diced tomatoes in juice
½ (6-oz) can tomato paste
2 dried red chiles, rehydrated in boiling water
Butter, as needed
3 hard-boiled eggs, halved
¼ c chopped parsley

Rinse rice in warm water until water runs clear. Drain very well.

In a 4-quart saucepan, warm 2 tablespoons oil over medium-high heat. Carefully add ¾ cup rice (it will splatter) and cook, stirring frequently, until rice begins to brown, about 5 minutes. Add remaining 2¼ cups rice, consommé, salt and enough water to cover rice by 1 inch. Reduce the heat so the mixture is at a gentle simmer, and cook for 1 hour.

Meanwhile, in a 10-inch skillet, warm remaining ¼ cup oil over medium heat. Add onion and sauté until transparent, about 3 minutes, stirring constantly. Stir in ham, tomatoes with juice, and tomato paste. Cover and cook over medium heat 10 minutes. Remove from heat, and reserve 1 cup of liquid from mixture.

When the rice has finished cooking, add tomato mixture. Squeeze rehydrated chiles over the saucepan, adding this chile juice into the cooked rice. (Discard chiles.) Stir to combine, cover with lid, and cook until tomato mixture is absorbed, about 3 minutes. (If rice is too dry, add a bit of reserved tomato liquid.)

Butter a 6- to 8-cup round mixing bowl. Arrange hard cooked eggs cut side down in bottom of bowl, and sprinkle with parsley. Add rice mixture, packing firmly into the bowl. Wait a few minutes, and then unmold onto a serving plate.

This dish is served in all West African countries.

Thai Tuna Salad . . . 174

Salads

FAITH ANDREWS BEDFORD

Faith Andrews Bedford is an author, writer, and volunteer for Meals On Wheels of Charlottesville/Albemarle.

Bombay Chicken Salad

SERVES 4

4 boneless, skinless chicken breasts
2 c chicken broth, plus more if needed
½ c light mayonnaise
½ tsp curry powder, plus more to taste
½ c mango chutney, finely chopped
¼ c plain yogurt
¼ tsp salt
⅛ tsp ground black pepper
1 large cucumber, peeled, seeded and chopped
2 hard-boiled eggs, peeled and chopped
1 head Boston lettuce, rinsed and patted dry
½ c raisins
2 scallions, finely chopped
½ c chopped peanuts

Place chicken breasts in medium pot. Add chicken broth to cover and bring to a boil over high heat. Cover with lid, reduce heat to medium-low, and simmer until chicken is cooked through and juices run clear when pierced with a fork, about 15 minutes. Drain chicken and transfer to a plate to cool. Chop cooled chicken into bite-size pieces.

In a large bowl, add mayonnaise, curry powder, chutney, yogurt, salt and pepper, and whisk together to combine. Add chicken, cucumber, and eggs, tossing until evenly coated with dressing.

To serve, line four plates with lettuce leaves and top with chicken salad. Sprinkle salad with raisins, scallions, and peanuts.

This is a low-fat summer salad with a touch of the Orient.

Tinsel Korey

Tinsel Korey is an actress, best known for her roles in the Twilight Saga films *New Moon* and *Eclipse*.

Grandma's Jell-O

SERVES 8 TO 10

2 c boiling water
1 (6-oz) pkg Lemon Jell-O
1 fresh banana, chopped
1 (11-oz) can mandarin oranges, drained
1 (8-oz) can pineapple chunks, drained
½ c chopped walnuts (optional)

In a large heat-proof bowl, add boiling water, and Jell-O, whisking to dissolve. Add 2 cups cold water, whisking to combine. Then, stir in bananas, mandarin oranges, pineapple chunks, and (optional) walnuts.

Refrigerate overnight to set. Serve.

Every Thanksgiving, there's one thing my family cannot live without—and that's Grandma's Jell-O. There's not even one spoonful left by the end of dinner. I wanted to share this recipe because it's quick, easy, and delicious. Enjoy it as much as we do.

Jim Waters

Jim Waters is the Director of Development for Meals On Wheels of Northampton County in Pennsylvania.

Shrimp Tortellini Salad

SERVES 4

½ c mayonnaise
1 Roma tomato, diced
½ c diced onion
1 stalk celery, diced
1 clove garlic, minced
1 tbsp white wine vinegar
1 tbsp freshly squeezed lemon juice
1 tbsp chopped parsley
1 tsp Italian seasoning
½ tsp Old Bay® seasoning
Dash of paprika
Salt and ground black pepper, to taste
1 (9-oz) pkg tricolor tortellini, cooked according to pkg directions, drained, and rinsed
½ lb peeled, deveined and cooked small shrimp

In a large bowl, combine all the ingredients except tortellini and shrimp. Mix dressing mixture well to combine.

Stir in the tortellini and shrimp into the dressing and mix well to coat. Serve chilled.

The kitchen staff recommended this recipe, originally introduced by one of our cooks, Pete Costalas, to be included on the menu for our Meals On Wheels' clients. However, the client services staff was reluctant to include it, doubting its receptivity among the seniors we serve. Yet it accidently appeared on the menu one week, and the feedback from our clients was overwhelmingly positive. Now, it has become a more frequent menu item, especially during the summer months.

Kurt and Brenda Warner

Former NFL quarterback and Super Bowl MVP Kurt Warner played for the St. Louis Rams, New York Giants, and Arizona Cardinals. His wife, Brenda Warner, is a Women of Faith speaker.

Lobster Pasta Salad

SERVES 4 TO 6

FOR THE DRESSING:
¾ c mayonnaise
1 c barbecue sauce
1 tbsp tarragon vinegar
Salt and ground black pepper, to taste

FOR THE SALAD:
6 oz orecchiette or small shell-shaped pasta, cooked according to pkg directions, drained and rinsed under cold water
2 c lobster meat, cut into bite-size chunks, taken from frozen lobster meat or 2 (1¼-lb) fresh lobsters
1 c diced celery
2 c shredded sharp cheddar cheese
½ c thinly-sliced scallions
2 tbsp chopped fresh tarragon or 2 tsp dried tarragon, crumbled

Make the dressing: In a small bowl, add dressing ingredients, and whisk together to combine. Season to taste with salt and pepper.

In a large bowl, add cooked pasta and remaining ingredients. Toss gently until well-mixed. Pour the dressing over salad and toss again gently.

Cover and refrigerate for at least 1 hour and up to 8 hours. If you refrigerate the salad for 8 hours or more, a small amount of mayonnaise may need to be added to moisten pasta salad. Serve chilled.

We always eat dinner together as a family—that's one rule that's rarely broken. If the kids want to have dinner with their friends, they're welcome to bring them to our house. But they all have to be home for dinner. Dinner comes with lots of rules, such as no one getting up from the table until the last person is finished eating. It's our way of telling the kids that each one is as important as the others, and nothing is more important than our family time. (Excerpt from First Things First: The Rules of Being a Warner, *published by Tyndale House Publishers, Inc., 2009.)*

Richard Karn

Richard Karn is an actor and TV personality, best known for his role in *Home Improvement* and as host of *Family Feud*.

Grandma Ruth's Shrimp Salad

SERVES 6

4 c finely-chopped Savoy cabbage
¾ c mayonnaise
1½ tbsp freshly squeezed lemon juice
1 tsp sugar
1 lb shrimp, peeled, deveined and cooked
¾ c chopped scallions
Salt and ground black pepper, to taste

In a large bowl, add cabbage. Add mayonnaise and stir until cabbage is evenly coated.

Stir in lemon juice, sugar, shrimp, and scallions. Season to taste with salt and pepper. Chill and serve.

My grandmother prepared this for the holidays, followed by my mother, and now I follow this same tradition by making it for all our special occasions.

WALTER NICHOLLS

Walter Nicholls is a food writer, who previously wrote for *The Washington Post*.

Thai Tuna Salad

MAKES 1½ CUPS

2 tsp finely chopped lemongrass (using only the inner core)
2 tsp peeled and finely chopped fresh gingerroot
1 tsp finely chopped kaffir lime leaves
1½ tbsp finely chopped white onion
2½ tbsp diced sweet red peppers
1 tsp finely chopped cilantro
2 tsp finely chopped scallions, green-part only
⅓ cup mayonnaise
1½ tsp freshly squeezed lime juice
A few drops hot sauce, like Tabasco, to taste
A few drops Worcestershire sauce, to taste
Pinch of ground black pepper and salt
1 tsp maple syrup
2 (5-oz) cans tuna, drained and finely shredded
Melba toasts, rice crackers, or sliced baguette, to serve

In a large bowl, combine all ingredients except tuna, and mix until well-blended.

Add the shredded tuna to the bowl and mix again. For the best flavor, cover, and refrigerate tuna for at least 2 hours prior to serving. Serve with accompaniments.

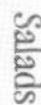

On a trip last year to Thailand, I awakened to a lost appreciation for, of all things—canned tuna. Every day at 6 p.m. Bangkok time, staff members of the legendary Mandarin Oriental deliver a small cocktail amenity to the hotel's orchid-filled guest rooms, placing the nibble beside the daily tropical fruit display. This hors d'oeuvre could be a coddled egg or, perhaps, a rich duck liver pâté. Another day, think sushi. One evening, a small pot of what looked like ho-hum tuna mush arrived. Not expecting much, I took a bite. It turned out to be an exceptional seafood spread with refreshing flavors that exploded in my mouth. Accented by notes of kaffir lime and lemongrass, it was made with one of Thailand's leading exports: a simple can of tuna. The recipe was created by hotel chef Enrico Froehnel.

A delicious way to eat your fill of Vitamin C and get strong!

LINDA BERNS

Linda Berns of CustomKosher, LLC, is a personal chef and caterer specializing in home-cooked kosher meals.

Popeye's Favorite Spinach Salad

SERVES 4-6

1 lb baby spinach
2 red Bartlett pears
1 thinly sliced red onion
1 pint grape tomatoes
1 c candied walnuts (recipe below)
1 c balsamic wine vinaigrette (recipe below)

Wash spinach well and strain in a colander or spin dry in a salad spinner. Refrigerate until ready to combine with other ingredients and toss salad.

Candy walnuts and make vinaigrette (recipes below).

Wash grape tomatoes and set aside. Do not refrigerate. Tomatoes lose their flavor when refrigerated.

Peel, wash, and thinly slice red onion and separate into rings. Set aside.

Wash pears. Set aside. Just before assembling, core and thinly slice pears into pieces about 2 inches long.

In a large bowl toss the spinach with pears, tomatoes, and red onions. Top with candied walnuts. Serve dressing on the side.

Balsamic Vinaigrette

¼ c balsamic vinegar
Little less than ¾ c extra virgin olive oil
3 tbsp water
2 tbsp white or brown sugar
1 to 2 tsp granulated garlic or ground garlic
½ tsp black pepper or to taste
Salt to taste

Combine vinegar, water, and spices in bowl and stir to combine.

Add extra virgin olive oil slowly and whisk. Serve dressing on the side of the salad.

Candied Walnuts

1 c shelled walnuts
Approximately ¼ c white sugar
An approximately 9- by 12-inch piece of foil or parchment taped on a counter top or table ready to receive the hot candied walnuts.

Put walnuts and sugar in a non-stick sauté pan over medium heat

Stir walnuts constantly with a wooden spoon or flexible spatula as the sugar melts/caramelizes and begins to coat the nuts. You may need to add more sugar to completely coat. Take care not to burn the sugar.

When the nuts are coated evenly, pour them onto secured foil or parchment on the counter to cool.

When the nuts have cooled break them apart for the salad and later use.

KEITH SNOW

Chef and cookbook author Keith Snow developed and launched Harvest Eating, a website and social network devoted to seasonal cooking.

Spinach Salad with Bacon Vinaigrette

SERVES 4

3 slices bacon
¼ c red onion, diced
1 clove garlic, minced
1 c medium mushrooms, sliced ¼-inch thick
1 tbsp finely chopped pecan
2 tbsp champagne vinegar
1 lb spinach, cleaned
1 c diced tomato
1 tbsp Dijon mustard
2 tbsp shredded Parmesan cheese
Salt and ground black pepper, to taste

In a large sauté pan over medium-high heat, add bacon and cook until crisp. Remove bacon from pan and transfer to a paper towel to drain.

Reduce heat to medium, adding onion and garlic to the pan with bacon fat. Cook until onions are soft and translucent, about 3 minutes. Add mushrooms and cook until softened, about 2 minutes. Add pecans and vinegar, and then season with salt and pepper. Add spinach, and cook, using tongs to toss spinach constantly, just until spinach is warm, about 30 seconds. Remove from heat.

Transfer spinach to a large bowl. Crumble the reserved bacon, and add to spinach along with the tomatoes, mustard, and Parmesan cheese. Toss until spinach is evenly coated. Season with salt and pepper, and serve.

This spinach salad celebrates an amazing season for being a local food advocate and chef—spring! In late spring, my spinach crop provides an abundant harvest that is very rewarding, as any avid gardener can attest. This salad is often enjoyed at my house during this time of abundance. The texture of the spinach mixed with the flavors of bacon, mustard, vinegar, and cheese are amazing on the palate. Use fresh garden-grown spinach and tomatoes, if possible.

Joan Lunden

Joan Lunden is a journalist, television host, and author. She was the co-host for *Good Morning America* for 17 years from 1980-1997.

Glitzy Glady's Potato Salad

From *Joan Lunden's Healthy Cooking* (Little, Brown and Company, 1997)

SERVES 10

3 lb red potatoes (12 to 14 medium), scrubbed
Salt and ground black pepper, to taste
⅓ c nonfat plain yogurt
⅓ c low-fat mayonnaise
2 tbsp Dijon mustard
2 tbsp cider or white wine vinegar
4 stalks celery, chopped
1 (3-oz) can sliced, pitted black olives
1 (4-oz) jar chopped pimentos, drained and rinsed
4 hard-boiled eggs minus 2 yolks, chopped
2 tbsp chopped scallions
3 tbsp chopped fresh parsley
Paprika, to garnish

Place potatoes in a saucepot with just enough water to cover. Season with salt, and bring to a boil over high heat. Cook potatoes until tender, about 20 to 25 minutes. Drain, and let potatoes cool until they can be handled. Cut into bite-size pieces, and reserve.

In a large bowl, whisk yogurt, mayonnaise, mustard, and vinegar. Season dressing with salt and pepper. Add potatoes and remaining ingredients, and toss well. Garnish with paprika, and serve.

My mom's famous for her potato salad. Since it was always one of my favorites, I had to include it in my book. I made a few changes from the original, such as cutting back on the number of egg yolks, which reduces the fat without tampering with the flavor. In this age of counting fat grams, if you use too many eggs, the yolk's on you. Recipe from Joan Lunden's Healthy Cooking, *published by Little, Brown and Company, 1997.*

Linda Berns

Linda Berns of CustomKosher, LLC, is a personal chef and caterer specializing in home-cooked kosher meals.

Mom's Moroccan Carrot Salad

SERVES 4-6

3 c thinly shredded carrots (approximately ½ to ¾ lb whole carrots)
¾ c black raisins
1 large naval orange (peeled and cut in ½-inch chunks)
¼ c extra virgin olive oil
¼ c preferably fresh orange juice
¼ tsp cinnamon
¼ tsp sugar
¼ tsp nutmeg (optional)
Salt & pepper to taste

Wash and peel carrots. Trim off ends.

Shred carrots on a grater or with the coarse shredder blade of a food processor and set aside.

Toss carrots with orange pieces and raisins in a medium bowl.

Combine olive oil, orange juice and spices in a bowl and whisk together.

Pour dressing over the carrot salad and toss. Adjust seasoning to taste.

Refrigerate to let flavors meld. Serve cold.

Everybody loves sweet carrots and raisins!

Mediterranean Stuffed Eggplant or Portobello Mushrooms . . . 208

Sides

Delilah Winder

Delilah Winder is a chef and entrepreneur. Her cooking has been featured on many national television food shows, including Food Network's *The Best of Southern Cuisine*, and CBS's *Chef On A Shoestring*.

I just can't help but smile and relax when I think about this dish. A steaming bowl of creamy stewed navy beans makes me happy any day of the week and at any time of year, but it is especially comforting in the winter, when all I want is something warm and satisfying. I remember playing outside in the snow as a little girl and seeing the kitchen window glowing and foggy from the steaming pot of beans cooking on the stove. Even then, I knew that I was happiest in the warm, fragrant kitchen. For me, this dish will also always represent Saturday night supper, especially in my pre-restaurant days when my family spent most Saturdays at home cleaning all day or fooling around with one hobby or another. I put the beans on the stove and, except for visiting the pot to give it a stir every so often, I pretty much left them alone. All day, the delicious aroma of those beans cooking made our stomachs growl, and we couldn't wait to sit at the table and dig in. A day can't get much better than that.

These beans are wonderful on their own, but they are even better with hearty bread or buttermilk biscuits, as I have suggested (opposite). Serve the biscuits on the side, or set a biscuit in your bowl and ladle the creamy beans overtop. If you want to add a bit of spice to the dish (and I always do), sprinkle some dried red pepper flakes over the beans; they will warm you up even more. Recipe from Delilah's Everyday Soul: Southern Cooking with Style, *published by Running Press, 2006.*

Stewed Navy Beans

SERVES 8

1 lb dried navy beans, thoroughly rinsed
4 (½-lb) ham hocks, scored or cracked, or 2 lb smoked turkey legs or wings, roughly chopped
1 c finely chopped yellow onion
¼ tsp dried oregano
¼ tsp dried thyme
2 dried bay leaves
1 tbsp finely chopped garlic
2 quarts chicken stock
1 tsp salt
Buttermilk biscuits, to serve

Place the beans in a large saucepan or Dutch oven and add just enough cold water to cover beans by about half an inch. Add the ham hocks or smoked turkey, onion, oregano, thyme, bay leaves, garlic, stock, and salt.

Bring mixture to a boil over medium-high heat. Continue to boil, stirring frequently, for about 20 minutes. Reduce heat to simmer. Cover and cook, stirring occasionally, until beans are tender and juices thicken, about 8 hours. Note that the beans will be very soft, appearing almost overcooked and ready to burst, but that's what you want. While cooking, add more water or stock as necessary just to keep the beans covered.

To serve, remove the bay leaves and discard. Transfer ham hocks or smoked turkey into a large serving bowl, or cut the meat from them and stir into the beans. Spoon beans into individual bowls and serve with biscuits.

James Denton

James Denton is an actor best known for his popular role on *Desperate Housewives*.

Cheese Grits Soufflé

SERVES 6

4 tbsp butter, plus more for greasing
2 c water
½ c quick-cooking grits
¼ c sharp cheddar cheese
¼ tsp salt
2 large eggs
⅓ c low-fat (1%) milk
¼ c freshly grated Parmesan cheese
Pinch of paprika (optional)

Preheat oven to 350°F. Use butter to grease a 2-quart baking dish or 4 (6-oz) ramekins.

Bring water to a boil in a 2-quart saucepot over medium-high heat. Reduce heat to low and gradually whisk in grits, continuing to whisk to eliminate any lumps. Cover the pot with a lid, and cook until water is absorbed and grits are creamy, about 10 minutes.

Remove from heat, and transfer grits to a large mixing bowl. Stir in butter, cheddar cheese, and salt until combined.

In separate small bowl, whisk eggs and milk together until combined, then add to grits, whisking until well-mixed. Pour entire mixture into prepared dish or ramekins. Sprinkle with Parmesan and (optional) paprika.

Bake uncovered in preheated oven, until top is golden and toothpick inserted in center comes out clean, about 45 to 60 minutes in baking dish and 30 minutes in ramekins. Serve immediately.

I believe there are very few substitutes for family mealtime together. It was the time that my family reconnected and caught up with everything going on in each other's lives. It's a great time for parents to take the pulse of their kids' social lives and get an early handle on conflict. Every night at the dinner table my kids have to tell me the best thing and worst thing about their day. And this Cheese Grits Soufflé is just one of many great recipes to have with that chat at the dinner table.

DON FRIESON

Don Frieson is an executive at Walmart.

Sweet & Tangy Memphis Barbecue Sauce

MAKES 2 CUPS

2 tbsp salted butter
1 small sweet onion, minced
2 garlic cloves, crushed
2 tbsp water
¼ c firmly-packed dark brown sugar
1 c ketchup
2 tbsp white vinegar
2 tbsp mustard, like yellow, Dijon, or honey mustard
2 tbsp Worcestershire sauce
1 tsp freshly grated orange zest
¼ c freshly squeezed orange juice (about 1 large orange)
Salt and ground black pepper, to taste
Cayenne powder, to taste

In a medium saucepan over low heat, melt butter. Add onion and garlic, and sauté until onion softens, about 5 minutes.

Gradually stir in water and brown sugar, and simmer for 1 minute. Stir in the remaining ingredients and continue to simmer over low heat for 20 minutes, stirring occasionally. Taste and adjust seasonings, as needed. Remove from heat, and let cool.

Store in the refrigerator for up to one week.

As a Memphis native, I appreciate good barbecue. This sauce is sure to please a crowd—it's great on pork, beef, poultry, or seafood. It can also be used as a dip for fresh vegetables or to flavor soups and savory side dishes. Save money, eat better!

LAURA SEN

Laura Sen is the president and CEO of BJ's Wholesale Club, a Fortune 500 membership warehouse retail store.

Mom's Cranberry-Orange Chutney

SERVES 6

1 (12-oz) bag fresh cranberries
2 unpeeled navel oranges, quartered
2 c sugar
1 c chopped walnuts (optional)

Add the berries into a food processor and briefly pulse just a couple of seconds at a time, until coarsely chopped. Don't over-process or the chutney will be mushy. Transfer the cranberries into a medium bowl and set aside.

Following the same directions as above, add the unpeeled, quartered oranges to the food processor, and briefly pulse just a couple of seconds at a time, until coarsely chopped. Don't over-process. Add to the medium bowl with the pulsed cranberries. (Note: For a sweeter chutney, grind the zest of one orange. Use a sharp paring knife or vegetable peeler and carefully peel off the orange's outer layer. Discard the bitter white pith and process the peeled sections together with the zest strips and unpeeled, quartered orange.)

Add sugar and walnuts (optional) into the bowl with the cranberries and oranges, stirring to combine. Cover tightly and refrigerate overnight to let flavors develop.

My mom made this every Thanksgiving in our tiny kitchen in Wakefield, Massachusetts. She always cooked for a couple dozen relatives. Looking back, what impresses me most is that, despite all of the challenges of preparing for the holiday, she still took the time and care to make her cranberry sauce—something most folks buy in a can—from scratch! Chutney is delicious served with pork, poultry, or sharp cheddar. It's great on English muffins, too! Just a tip—this is best prepared at least one day in advance so the flavor has time to develop.

Jerusalem Artichoke Gratin

SERVES 8 TO 10

1 tbsp butter, softened
6 c thinly-sliced Jerusalem artichokes (about 2½ lb), scrubbed, peeled and thinly-sliced
1 large onion, sliced
½ lb Swiss or Havarti cheese, grated
1 c heavy cream
Salt and ground black pepper, to taste
Parmesan cheese, for sprinkling (optional)

Preheat oven to 350°F.

Butter a large casserole dish. Line the bottom of the dish evenly with half the Jerusalem artichokes. Spread evenly and top with half the onions and half the Swiss cheese. Sprinkle with salt and pepper and repeat with the remaining artichokes, onions and Swiss cheese, ending with cheese. (Depending on the size of the casserole dish, you may have 2 or 3 layers.)

Add cream, pouring it evenly over the gratin. Sprinkle with Parmesan cheese and bake until artichokes are fork-tender, about 30 minutes.

Cokie Roberts

Cokie Roberts is an Emmy Award–winning journalist and bestselling author. She's also a contributing senior news analyst on NPR and a political commentator for ABC News.

Family dinners have always been a big part of our lives, especially the hallowed tradition of Sunday night dinner when several generations often come together. We also celebrate big meals with cousins and the in-laws of in-laws, especially around the holidays. For Christmas, we usually have about 50 people and, in addition to the turkey and goose, there's one vegetable we always serve, but the recipe has changed dramatically over the years.

When I was growing up, my family often spent Christmas at a great-uncle's in Pointe Coupee Parish, Louisiana. There my father, an avid gardener, collected some Jerusalem artichoke roots and planted them in the backyard of our home in suburban Washington, DC, more than 50 years ago. My husband and I still live in that house, and every year we dig up those artichokes right before Christmas.

I used to boil them until soft and then mash them in a food processor with butter, cream, salt, and pepper. I thought that dish was delicious but the younger generation whined about the "yucky green stuff." Since I essentially treated the tubers (now often called "sunchokes") as potatoes, I decided I could make a gratin instead. Success! Everyone loves the dish and best of all—I don't have to make it anymore. Now the whole family contributes a dish or two to the dinner, and my stellar son-in-law has taken over the artichoke duties.

Not only is this dish delicious, I love the fact that even after my father who planted them and my great-uncle who inspired them are long gone, the artichokes live on, keeping us connected to our family through the generations.

Linda Berns

Linda Berns of CustomKosher, LLC, is a personal chef and caterer specializing in home-cooked kosher meals.

Kale & Sweet Potatoes

SERVES 4

1 medium large bunch of kale (approximately ¾ lb)
3 to 4 medium sweet potatoes
4 tbsp olive oil
3 tbsp balsamic or sherry vinegar
Salt and ground black pepper, to taste

Remove the kale leaves from the hard center stems. Tear leaves in large bite size pieces.

Soak leaves in large bowl of water while you peel the sweet potatoes and cut them into approximately 2-inch chunks.

Boil sweet potatoes until just tender as you assemble all the other ingredients.

When just tender, drain the sweet potatoes and set aside.

Drain kale leaves in colander and set aside.

Add olive oil to large skillet or sauté pan over medium high heat.

Add kale and stir to coat with oil. Continue tossing and stirring kale just until it turns bright green and becomes tender.

Add sweet potato chunks to kale and toss.

Add balsamic or sherry vinegar to pan and toss to coat kale and potatoes.

Season with salt and pepper to taste. Serve hot.

Eat as a healthy side dish with fish, chicken or beef.

Carrie Crowell

Carrie Crowell is the granddaughter of legendary singer Johnny Cash, daughter of Roseanne Cash. She hosts an online cooking show, Big City Grits, which has been featured in the Wall Street Journal and on the Cooking Channel.

The original recipe for this squash casserole came from my great grandmother, Mrs. Carrie Cash, who I am named after. My mother learned this recipe from Grandma Carrie, and in turn passed it down to my three sisters and me. My sister Chelsea adds Tabasco sauce; our mom thinks that's disgusting, but I can't quite tell the difference. Adaptations and experimentation are a part of the learning process and I think my great grandmother would be proud of how well-loved and ardently-debated her recipe is.

Great Grandma Carrie's Squash Casserole

SERVES 8

5 unpeeled yellow squash, cubed
1 white onion, chopped
1 stick (½ c) unsalted butter
1½ c whole milk
2 eggs
2 c grated sharp cheddar cheese
2 c crumbled Saltine crackers
Salt and ground black pepper, to taste

Begin by boiling cubed squash for 5 to10 minutes at medium to high heat, making sure the squash stays slightly undercooked (it will cook further in the oven).

In a skillet, sauté chopped onions with one stick of butter at medium heat until the onions turn translucent.

In a large mixing bowl, combine milk and eggs and whisk together thoroughly. Add 1 cup of grated cheese, 1 cup of crushed crackers, salt and pepper, and stir together.

Once onions and squash have both cooled, combine them with the milk and egg mixture and stir. (It is important that the squash and onions have cooled so they don't cook the egg).

Pour mixture into a baking dish or casserole pan, and sprinkle 1 cup of crackers on top along with 1 cup of grated sharp cheddar.

Bake at 400°F for about 30 minutes, or until the top is golden brown.

LINDA BERNS

Linda Berns of CustomKosher, LLC, is a personal chef and caterer specializing in home-cooked kosher meals.

Colorful, Low-Calorie, Curry Cauliflower

SERVES 4-6

1 medium cauliflower
1 large diced onion
3 peeled and finely shredded carrots (approximately 1 c)
4 to 5 tbsp olive oil
3 tbsp minced garlic – preferably fresh
1 (14- to 16-oz) can diced tomatoes
2 tbsp curry powder, or to taste
½ tsp cumin, or to taste
Salt and ground black pepper, to taste

Wash and peel carrots. Trim off ends. Shred on the fine end of a grater or with the fine blade of a food processor and set aside.

Wash and break cauliflower into medium size florettes and set aside.

Peel, wash and chop onion to a medium dice.

Add oil to pan over medium heat.

Add onions and garlic to pan and stir occasionally.

When onions begin to turn golden add cauliflower and toss to coat with remaining oil.

Add curry, cumin, and season lightly with salt and pepper. Toss and cook for approximately 5 minutes. Cauliflower should only begin to soften at this stage.

Add diced tomatoes and their juice to pan, and let simmer until cauliflower is tender but not mushy.

Adjust seasoning to taste. Garnish with chopped scallions or parsley and serve hot.

Eat as a side dish with a main course protein, or as a main course with rice, quinoa, or couscous.

YVETTE NICOLE BROWN

Yvette Nicole Brown is an actress and comedienne, best known for her role as Shirley Bennett in *Community*. She has also appeared on *Malcolm in the Middle*, *That's So Raven*, and *Drake & Josh*.

Mom's Green Bean Delight

SERVES 6 TO 8

4 (14.5-oz) cans French-style or regular green beans, drained
2 (14.5-oz) cans whole kernel corn, drained, or 1 (16-oz) bag frozen corn
2 to 3 (14-oz) cans 99% fat free chicken broth
1¾ c water, as needed
1 onion, quartered
3 to 5 lb Idaho potatoes, peeled and quartered (1 to 2 medium potatoes per person)
Lemon pepper, to taste
Granulated garlic, to taste
Salt and ground black pepper, to taste
Cornbread and salad, to serve

In a large, nonstick pot, combine all ingredients. Bring to a boil over high heat and cook until potatoes are fork-tender, about 25 to 30 minutes. (The potatoes will thicken the broth.)

Remove from heat, and serve with cornbread and salad.

That fancy name is what my mom came up with for the purposes of this cookbook. All my life I've simply called it "that deliciously awesome dish my mom makes with green beans," but I guess that's a little long. This dish is special to me because it reminds me of my mom and of home. It's quick and easy to make but so good, and I hope you all enjoy it. Also, to make this a complete meal in a pot, consider adding ham chunks to the mix.

Jean Sagendorph

Jean Sagendorph is an author (*Starry Night, Hold Me Tight* published by Running Press, and *The Ice Box Cookbook* published by Chronicle Books) and a literary agent. She lives in NYC with her husband, Sam Pocker, and two ridiculous cats.

I love my Mom dearly, and she's a fantastic cook, but she made one tragic error. When I was a child, she would encourage me to eat boiled Brussels sprouts by referring to them as "mini cabbages." I hate cabbage. The smell makes me run far away. I refused these "mini cabbages" for years. On the occasion of my fortieth birthday, my husband gathered my closest friends and took us to one of my favorite restaurants in NYC. A few glasses of wine later, a mixed plate of hors d'oeuvres was placed on the table. Among the assemblage, Brussels sprouts. Perhaps it was the wine or my fear of hitting forty but I announced to everyone that I was going to eat my first Brussels sprout ever. I popped it in my mouth and instantly fell in love.

My husband says that my eyes popped out of my head. Cabbage? No! More like a wonderfully roasted french fry. Who knew? So many years lost! After that birthday dinner, I quite literally made Brussels sprouts every night for several weeks. People started to tease me on Facebook and Twitter. I was a woman consumed. I made the roasted version for my mom (she always boiled) and she was floored too; she loved them.

Roasted Brussels Sprouts

SERVES 2 TO 3 (UNLESS YOU ARE ME, THEN IT SERVES 1!)

1 (10-oz) pkg fresh Brussels sprouts
1 tbsp olive oil, divided
½ tsp course sea salt, or Kosher salt
⅓ tsp ground black pepper

Preheat the oven to 400°F.

Remove any wilted leaves from the Brussels sprouts and cut each Brussels sprout in half. If they are larger than a walnut, cut them in quarters. Placed the cut sprouts into a medium bowl. Pour ¾ tablespoon olive oil into the bowl and gently stir the sprouts around, so they get a shiny coating of oil.

Line a baking sheet with parchment paper. Transfer the Brussels sprouts to the cookie sheet, pushing the sprouts around, so that they are in a single layer with a bit of room around each piece. Sprinkle the remaining ¼ tablespoon olive oil on the sprouts, along with salt and pepper.

Place the cookie sheet in the oven, and roast for 25 minutes. Using a wooden spoon move the sprouts around, so that they brown evenly. Roast for an additional 15 to 20 minutes. Season with additional salt to taste. If you want to get really wild, mix in small chunks of crispy bacon. Serve.

Chris Frantz

Chris Frantz is a music producer and musician. He was the drummer for the bands Talking Heads and Tom Tom Club.

Potatoes au Gratin

SERVES 6

2 tbsp butter
1 tbsp minced garlic
2 lb Yukon Gold potatoes, peeled and thinly sliced
Salt and ground black pepper
1 sweet yellow onion, finely chopped
2½ c grated Gruyere cheese, divided
1 c cooked and coarsely chopped bacon (about ½ lb)
2 tbsp chopped parsley
Cream, as needed

Preheat oven to 350°F. Rub a 9- by 12-inch gratin dish with butter and crushed garlic.

Make one layer of sliced potatoes overlapping like shingles on a roof in the bottom of the dish. Season with salt and freshly ground black pepper. Then, add a layer of finely chopped yellow onions and 1 cup of cheese atop the potatoes. Sprinkle with the bacon and parsley.

Add a second layer of the sliced potatoes. Season with salt and pepper, and add a top layer of remaining 1 cup Gruyere. Gently pour light cream over the dish until the top layer of potatoes is almost covered.

Bake in the preheated oven for 30 minutes, and flatten the top layer with a metal spatula to keep au gratin moist. Cook until the gratin is a golden brown and the potatoes are cooked (insert a knife in the gratin to check them), about 30 more minutes. Sprinkle the top with another layer of Gruyere for the last 15 minutes of baking. Remove from oven, and serve.

This dish is a total crowd pleaser. It is comfort food at its best. I use Yukon Gold potatoes because they do not fall apart when baking. The potatoes need to be thinly sliced to about 1/8 of an inch. You can use a mandoline, but I just do it by hand with a good sharp chopping knife.

Linda Berns

Linda Berns of CustomKosher, LLC, is a personal chef and caterer specializing in home-cooked kosher meals.

Mediterranean Stuffed Eggplant or Portobello Mushrooms

SERVES 4 AS SIDE DISH OR 2 AS A MAIN COURSE

1 medium eggplant cut in half lengthwise; remove the meat, leave the shell intact, and set aside
2 large zucchini, diced into approximately ⅜-inch pieces
2 large yellow squash, diced into approximately ⅜-inch pieces
1 (24-oz) can diced tomatoes, with juice
8 oz fresh mushrooms, wiped clean, stem tips removed; cut in large pieces
2 c diced onions
2 to 3 tbsp chopped garlic
¼ to ½ c olive oil, as needed
¼ c wine—red or white whatever is on hand (optional)
8 oz firm tofu, cut into approximately ½-inch cubes (optional)
½ to ¾ c mozzarella or feta cheese (optional)
1 tsp sugar to taste
1 tsp kosher salt
¼ tsp course ground black pepper
Additional salt and ground black pepper, to taste

Dice eggplant meat into approximately ½-inch cubes.

Fry eggplant cubes in 4 tablespoons of olive oil in a sauté pan over medium heat. Stir frequently to brown evenly. You may have to add extra olive oil. When brown remove from pan and set aside in a large bowl.

Brown onions and 2 tablespoons of garlic together in sauté pan with another 3 or 4 tablespoons of olive oil over medium heat. Cook until onions begin to turn golden.

Add diced tomatoes and juice, sautéed eggplant, wine, sugar, kosher salt, and black pepper to the pan. Bring to a boil, and then turn down to a simmer. Let sauce simmer uncovered until most of the liquid is reduced.

Add trimmed and quartered button mushrooms. Continue to let simmer 5 minutes. Adjust seasoning and remove from heat.

Mix sauce with uncooked and diced squash and tofu in a large bowl.

Spread the saved 1 tablespoon of ground garlic and drizzle 1 tablespoon of olive oil around the inside of each half of the eggplant shell.

Fill the shells with the vegetable stuffing and top with mozzarella or feta cheese (optional)

Bake in oven preheated to 375°F until the cheese is melted, the yellow and green squash turn bright colors, and the stuffed eggplants are hot throughout—approximately 20 minutes.

To make stuffed Portobello mushrooms follow the steps preceding, then:

Remove the stem of the Portobello mushroom cap. Delicately scoop out the black hairy underside to create a well for the filling.

Spread the pureed garlic and drizzle olive oil on the underside of each cap and fill with the stuffing mixture.

Top with cheese.

Line a baking dish large enough to hold all the mushrooms with foil and spread another 1 tablespoon of olive oil around the bottom.

Place the mushrooms in the pan.

Mushrooms should bake at 400°F until the cheese is melted, the yellow and green squash turn bright colors, and the stuffed eggplants are hot throughout—approximately 15 minutes.

Hardy and heart healthy all year round!

Mandelbrodt . . . 233

Desserts

continued on back . . .

DEB MCLEAN

Deb McLean is the Nutrition Director of the Community Meals Program at Somerville-Cambridge Elder Service in Massachusetts.

Carrot Nut Raisin Cookies

MAKES 10 DOZEN

3⅔ c all-purpose flour
1½ c sugar
1½ tsp baking soda
1½ tsp allspice
¼ tsp ground cloves
½ c canola oil
1 egg (if substituting egg, add ¼ c oil instead)
2 (4-oz) jars carrot baby food
1½ c walnuts
1½ c raisins

Preheat oven to 375°. Prepare cookie sheets by lightly oiling them.

In a large bowl, mix the flour, sugar, baking soda, and spices. Add the wet ingredients—canola oil, egg, and baby food. Mix by hand until well-blended. Stir in nuts and raisins.

Drop cookie mixture onto cookie sheet by rounded teaspoon, 2 inches apart.

Bake cookies for 8 minutes or until brown in preheated oven. Remove cookies to wire racks to cool.

I developed this recipe in college. My goal was to determine the acceptability of cookies made with vegetables and to assess resultant cookie quality using ratings by adolescents. However, seniors love them too. The recipe can be made without egg for vegans.

ELLEN LAMBERT

Ellen Lambert is an executive with The Merck Company Foundation.

Renee's Apple Cake

SERVES 12

Butter, to grease pan
2½ c sugar, divided
¼ c cinnamon
3 c all-purpose flour
3 tsp baking powder
1 c oil
4 eggs
¼ c orange juice
2½ tsp vanilla extract
6 to 8 medium Granny Smith apples, peeled and thinly-sliced

Preheat oven to 350°F. Grease and flour a Bundt pan or angel food pan with butter.

In a small bowl, stir ½ cup sugar and cinnamon together. Set aside.

In a medium bowl, add flour, 2 cups sugar and baking powder together, and mix. Gradually mix in oil, eggs, orange juice and vanilla until smooth.

Pour one-third of the batter into prepared tube pan. Spread half of the sliced apples on top of batter and sprinkle with half of the cinnamon sugar. Pour half of the remaining batter over apples and spread remaining apples on top of batter. Sprinkle with remaining cinnamon sugar.

Top with remaining batter and bake in preheated oven for 1 hour and 15 minutes, or until a toothpick inserted in the center of the cake comes out clean. Remove cake from oven and cool on a wire rack.

My mother and father live in a small apartment housed in a huge apartment complex near where my dad works. Yup, eighty-five and still working. This is a big change from the large house we grew up in and it is quite a distance from the old friends and family who were always around. But an apartment complex has riches in all of the potential friendships that can develop on a walk to the mailbox, a stroll to get the newspaper, or the ring of the doorbell. Renee and her dog, Cookie, lived across the hall from my parents. Renee introduced herself one morning by bringing over a piece of her "famous" apple cake on her way to walk Cookie. She was warm and friendly, and so was her cake. Instant friendship was formed. By baking for her neighbors and inviting them over for coffee and cake, Renee created a community of supportive, sharing, caring friends. These neighbors also became family friends, attending weddings, celebrating holidays and birthdays (they ranged in age from twenty-five to eighty-five years old), and supporting each other through sadder events as well. This delicious cake brings the warmth of neighbors and friends close, starting with the aroma and ending with each delicious bite. Serve warm or cold. Also, this makes excellent breakfast toast.

Gretchen Carlson

Gretchen Carlson is a TV personality, currently co-hosting *Fox & Friends* and previously co-anchoring *The Early Show*. A former Miss America winner, she is the national spokesperson for March of Dimes.

Mom's Crème de Menthe Cake

SERVES 12 (THIS CAKE SERVES A BIG FAMILY!)

FOR THE CAKE:
1 c vegetable oil, plus more to grease pan
1 (18-oz) yellow cake mix
1 (4-oz) box pistachio instant pudding mix
4 tbsp Crème de Menthe plus enough water to make 1 cup
4 eggs
A few drops green food coloring
¼ c chocolate syrup

FOR THE FROSTING:
3 tbsp butter
3 tbsp milk (skim, 2%, or whole)
3 oz semi-sweet chocolate chips
3 oz milk chocolate chips

Make the cake: Preheat oven to 350°F. Grease a Bundt pan with vegetable oil.

Mix together cake mix, pudding mix, oil, Crème de Menthe-water mixture, and eggs together with an electric mixer on low speed until smooth and combined. Add a few drops green food coloring to make the batter bright green. Add two-thirds of the batter to prepared pan. Add in chocolate syrup to remaining batter, and mix well. Pour this chocolate batter over green batter. Drag a knife through the batter to marble it.

Bake cake in preheated oven 45 minutes to 1 hour, until a toothpick inserted in center of cake comes out clean. Do not over-bake. Remove from oven and cool 20 minutes. Invert cake onto a platter.

Make the frosting: In a small saucepot, add butter and milk. Bring to a boil over high heat, boiling just 1 minute. Remove from heat and stir in the chocolate chips until they melt and frosting is smooth. Add more milk if frosting is too thick. Drizzle frosting over cooled cake.

Growing up in Minnesota, I was lucky enough to have all of my immediate relatives live within a mile of our home. Consequently, we entertained my grandparents, aunts, uncles, and cousins often for lunch and dinner. We always got together for birthdays, too, and I had a favorite cake—my mom's infamous Crème de Menthe concoction! Ok, I admit it. I'm a chocoholic. I requested it every June for my birthday, and I still request it when I go home to Minnesota to visit. I'm no Julia Child in the kitchen, but even I can make this cake almost as well as my mom. Here's a secret tip before serving: warm the cake in the microwave and put a dollop of vanilla ice cream on each slice.

JIM WATERS

Jim Waters is the Director of Development for Meals On Wheels of Northampton County in Pennsylvania.

The Best & Easiest Chocolate Cake

SERVES 12 TO 16

FOR THE CAKE:
2 c all-purpose flour
2 c sugar
1 c vegetable or canola oil
2 tsp baking soda
1 c hot coffee
1 c 2% milk
¾ c cocoa powder
2 eggs
1 tsp baking powder
1 tsp cream of tartar
1 tsp vanilla extract

FOR THE ICING:
1 stick (½ c) butter or margarine, melted
⅔ c cocoa powder
3 c confectioners' sugar
⅓ c milk
1 tsp vanilla extract

Make the cake: Preheat oven to 350°F. Lightly grease a 13- by 9-inch pan with nonstick cooking spray and then flour the pan.

In a large mixing bowl, add all ingredients. Beat with an electric mixer until well-mixed, about 5 minutes. Pour batter into prepared pan and bake until a toothpick inserted in center of cake comes out clean, 25 to 30 minutes. Let cool.

Make the icing: Place melted butter in a medium bowl. Stir in the cocoa powder. Then, alternately add confectioners' sugar, and milk, beating with an electric mixer to make light and fluffy Add additional milk, 1 tablespoon at a time, if too stiff. Stir in vanilla. Use to frost the cooled chocolate cake.

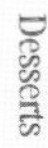

This cake is so moist and, even better, is the easiest chocolate cake to make. I have made it for company and brought it to parties—it's always a real hit. The icing recipe is adapted from Hershey's Perfectly Chocolate Cake recipe.

Joseph Lieberman

Joseph Lieberman is the United States senator from Connecticut.

Marcia Lieberman's Honey Cake

SERVES 12 TO 16

3 c flour
2 tsp baking powder
1½ tsp baking soda
1 c sugar
1 c honey
1 c water
½ c vegetable oil
3 eggs
1 tsp brandy
¾ c chopped walnuts (optional)

Preheat oven to 350°F . Lightly coat a 10-inch tube or Bundt pan with nonstick cooking spray.

In a large bowl, sift flour, baking powder, and baking soda together.

Add sugar, honey, water, oil, eggs, and brandy in bowl of an electric mixer and beat together until well-blended. Gradually add sifted, dry ingredients, and mix until thoroughly combined. Fold in (optional) nuts.

Pour batter into prepared pan and bake until toothpick inserted in center of cake comes out clean, about 1 hour. Remove from oven, and let cool.

This is a recipe for my mother's honey cake, one of my favorite family recipes. You may also throw in some nuts of your choice; Marcia used walnuts.

Mark Pryor

Mark Pryor is the United States senator from Arkansas, having previously served as the attorney general of Arkansas and as a representative in the Arkansas House of Representatives.

Susie Pryor's Scotch Fudge Cake

SERVES 12 TO 16

FOR THE CAKE:
2 sticks (1 c) margarine
1 c water
3 tbsp cocoa powder
2 c flour
2 c sugar
½ c buttermilk
2 large eggs
1 tsp baking soda
1 tsp ground cinnamon
1 tsp vanilla extract

FOR THE ICING:
1 stick (½ c) margarine
6 tbsp whole milk
3 tbsp cocoa powder
1 box (3¾ c) confectioners' sugar
1 tsp vanilla extract

Make the cake: Preheat oven to 375°F. Coat a 13- by 9- by 2-inch baking dish with nonstick cooking spray.

In a medium pot, add margarine, water, and cocoa powder and warm over medium heat until butter melts. Whisk to combine, and remove from heat.

In a large bowl, combine flour, sugar, buttermilk, eggs, baking soda, cinnamon, and vanilla extract until well-mixed. Add margarine mixture and beat until just combined. Pour batter into prepared pan and bake in preheated oven for 20 to 25 minutes, or until cake pulls away from the sides of the pan. Cool.

Make the icing: In a medium pot, combine margarine, milk and cocoa powder and bring to a boil over medium heat. Add confectioners' sugar and vanilla, stirring until sugar dissolves and icing is smooth, about 2 minutes. Pour hot icing over cake.

My favorite food is my grandmother, Susie Pryor's, Scotch Fudge Cake. There is no telling how many of these cakes my grandmother has made over the years. She always added nuts, but it is a winner with or without them. I hope you enjoy.

Mya Greene

Mya Greene is the director for the Habersham County Senior Center.

Big Gran's Sour Cream Pound Cake

SERVES 16 TO 20

3 c all-purpose flour (or cake flour)
¼ tsp baking soda
1 c sour cream
1 tbsp buttermilk
3 sticks (1½ c) salted butter
3 c sugar
1 tbsp vanilla extract
1 tbsp almond extract
6 large eggs
Juice of 1 lemon

Preheat oven to 325°F. Grease and flour a standard size tube pan, knocking out excess flour.

In a medium bowl, sift flour and baking soda together. In a small bowl, mix sour cream and buttermilk.

In a large bowl with an electric mixer, add butter and sugar, and beat together until creamy, about 8 minutes. Add in extracts and add eggs, one at a time, beating well after each addition. Add lemon juice, and mix again to combine.

With the mixer at low speed, add flour and sour cream/buttermilk mixture alternately in batches to butter mixture, beating until just combined.

Pour batter into prepared tube pan and bake for 1 hour and 25 minutes, or until toothpick inserted in center comes out clean. Remove from oven, cool cake in pan for 15 minutes and turn out onto rack to cool completely.

My grandmother shared this recipe with me when I was sixteen years old (I'm fifty-six now) and told me it was her favorite pound cake recipe. She said it was her favorite not only because of its wonderful taste and texture but also because she had changed the ingredients over the years until she thought it was perfect. I made this cake for the first time for Christmas 1996. I couldn't believe it had taken me that long because it brought back so many wonderful memories, like smelling the delightful aroma while it was baking, and tasting that delicious flavor that was so much a memory of my granny. Thank you, Big Gran.

This recipe for an Italian fruit cake called Panforte is more like candy than cake. The governor and her family enjoy making this recipe together.

Nikki Haley

Nikki Haley is the governor of South Carolina. The first female governor of South Carolina, Haley previously served in the South Carolina House of Representatives for five years.

Panforte (Italian Fruit Cake)

MAKES 16 WEDGES

Butter, for greasing
4 tsp cocoa powder, plus additional for dusting
⅔ c all-purpose flour
1 tsp ground cinnamon
½ tsp ground ginger
⅛ tsp ground cloves
¼ teaspoon salt
1 c whole almonds, toasted
1 c whole walnuts, toasted
1 c dried figs, diced
1 c dried blueberries
1 c dried apricot, diced
¾ c granulated sugar
⅔ c honey
Confectioners' sugar, as needed

Preheat oven to 300°F.

Line a springform pan with parchment paper. Grease paper well with butter and dust with cocoa powder.

In a large bowl, whisk together flour, spices, salt, and cocoa. Then, stir in nuts and dried fruit.

In a 2-quart heavy saucepan over moderate heat, bring granulated sugar and honey to a boil, stirring until sugar is dissolved. Let sugar mixture boil—without stirring—until a candy thermometer registers between 238°F to 240°F, about 2 minutes.

Immediately pour sugar over fruit mixture and quickly stir until combined (mixture will be very thick and sticky). Quickly spoon mixture into the springform pan, spreading the mixture evenly.

Bake in preheated oven 50 to 55 minutes. Remove from oven, and cool panforte completely in pan on a rack, then remove side of pan and invert, peeling off paper. Sprinkle with confectioners' sugar. To serve, cut with a serrated knife into small pieces.

OJ and Chanda Brigance

OJ Brigance was a special teams NFL player and a member of the 2001 Super Bowl champion Baltimore Ravens. Brigance and his wife Chanda are the founders of the Brigance Brigade Fund, a foundation that raises money to improve the quality of life, support treatment for, and fund research for ALS (or Lou Gehrig's disease), which Brigance was diagnosed with in 2007.

Cream Cheese Pound Cake

SERVES 12

3 c all-purpose flour
Pinch of salt
3 sticks butter (1½ c), softened
1 (8-oz) pkg cream cheese, softened
3 c sugar
6 large eggs
½ c milk
1 tsp vanilla extract
1 tsp lemon juice

Preheat oven to 325°F. Grease and flour a standard size tube pan.

In a large bowl, sift flour and salt together 3 times. Set aside.

Add butter and cream cheese to a large bowl, using an electric mixer to cream together until smooth. Gradually add sugar and mix until light and fluffy. Add eggs one at a time, beating well after each addition, and beat until creamy. Add sifted flour and milk, alternately, beginning and ending with flour, mixing on low to combine. Add vanilla and lemon juice, and beat until smooth.

Pour batter into prepared tube pan and bake in preheated oven for 1 hour and 15 minutes. Remove from oven, and cool.

Meals On Wheels has been providing delicious, well-balanced meals for senior citizens for years. Their services allow seniors to retain their independence and have a better quality of life. That is why we support Meals On Wheels: They deliver a little love to every doorstep.

Paul Fitzpatrick

Paul Fitzpatrick is the president and COO of RLTV, having previously worked for other major broadcast organizations, including Hallmark Entertainment, The Weather Channel, C-SPAN, The Golf Channel. Fitzpatrick also worked in the United States Senate, House of Representatives, and in the White House Office of Telecommunications Policy.

Betty's Five-Flavor Cake

SERVES 12 TO 16

FOR THE CAKE:
2 sticks (1 c) butter
½ c vegetable or canola oil
3 c sugar
5 large eggs, beaten
3 c all-purpose flour
½ tsp baking powder
1 tsp coconut extract
1 tsp rum extract
1 tsp butter extract
1 tsp lemon extract
1 tsp vanilla extract
1 tsp almond extract
1 c whole milk

FOR THE GLAZE:
½ c sugar
¼ c water
1 tsp butter extract
1 tsp coconut extract
1 tsp rum extract
1 tsp almond extract
1 tsp lemon extract
1 tsp vanilla extract

Make the cake: Preheat oven to 350°F. Grease and flour a 10-inch tube or Bundt pan.

In the bowl of an electric mixer, add butter, oil, and sugar, and cream together until light and fluffy. Add eggs one at a time, mixing well after each addition.

In a medium bowl, whisk flour and baking powder together. Slowly stir in flour and milk, alternately, to butter mixture, beginning and ending with flour. Stir in extracts and pour batter into prepared pan.

Bake for 1½ hours, or until toothpick inserted into center of cake comes out clean. Remove from oven and place on a wire rack to cool.

Make the glaze: In a small pot, combine sugar, water, butter, coconut extract, and rum extract, and bring to a boil over medium heat. Remove from heat and cool slightly. Stir in almond, lemon, and vanilla extracts. Return to a boil, and then pour over cake. Cover the cake with foil and cool. Remove cake from pan before serving.

This is an amazingly great family cake, fun for get-togethers and birthday parties.

Penny Pollack

Penny Pollack is the dining editor for *Chicago Magazine*.

I learned how to make mandelbrodt the old-fashioned way—frantically following my grandfather-in-law around his kitchen, measuring his handfuls of flour, and scribbling down everything he said and did as he mixed, kneaded, and shaped the sticky dough into four oven-ready loaves, as easily as a child rolls Play-Doh into whimsical shapes. The dear man had been making the stuff since before he got off the boat, and he had no use for pesky details like measurements and instructions. The first few times I soloed, more dough wound up on my hands and arms then on the cookie sheets, but I persevered until I got it right. These days, I can have the raw dough ready for baking in 20 minutes flat—except when my grandchildren "help" me.

Some forty-five years after my first mandelbrodt-baking lesson, I'm delighted to share this Old World recipe—complete with my dough-handling tips—with you. I hope that mandelbrodt will become a favorite treat to pair with coffee for your family, as it is for mine. I like to keep all the ingredients on hand, as this is the perfect recipe for a rainy or snow-bound day.

Mandelbrodt

MAKES 50 TO 60 COOKIES (ENOUGH TO FILL A NORMAL-SIZED COOKIE TIN)

4 eggs
1 c plus 2 tbsp sugar
1 c vegetable oil
1 tbsp lemon juice
3½ c all-purpose flour
2 tsp baking powder
Pinch of ground orange rind
2 (2-oz) pkg slivered almonds, roughly chopped
Shortening, as needed
Cinnamon-sugar

Preheat oven to 325°F.

Mix eggs, 1 cup sugar, and vegetable oil together in a medium bowl until well blended. Stir in lemon juice.

In a separate bowl, combine flour, baking powder, and orange rind. Add flour to egg mixture gradually, about one-third at a time, blending well after each addition. Add almonds and mix until well-blended. The dough should be thick and sticky to handle.

Shape dough into loaves: Since this dough is very pliable, if you mess up, you can reshape it and try again. Use shortening to grease your butter knife blade and your hands to keep dough from sticking. Scoop one-fourth of the dough and gently toss it back and forth between your well-greased hands until you have a smooth, torpedo-shaped mass. Lay the dough down lengthwise on one side of a baking sheet and gently stretch it until it's about 14½-inches long.

Pat the dough gently with your fingertips until it's about 4 inches wide. These loaves are not meant to be perfect rectangles. Cup your hand around each end to round out the top and bottom. Repeat with the remaining dough until you have 2 baking sheets with 2 loaves on each.

Sprinkle each loaf lightly with cinnamon-sugar and bake for 25 minutes. Remove from oven and lower oven temperature to 275°F. The loaves will not be baked through.

Using a serrated knife, gently slice each loaf on the diagonal into ½-inch to ¾-inch wide pieces. Separate the pieces on the baking sheets, so there is a little space between each slice. (If you don't want to use your knife on your baking sheets, cut each loaf in half and slide onto a cutting board. Then arrange the pieces back on the baking pans as instructed above.)

Place mandelbrodt back in the oven and bake 1½ to 2 hours, until the loaves are completely baked through and golden brown, a process which cannot be rushed. Remove from oven, and let cool.

Peter Marshall

Peter Marshall was the original host of *The Hollywood Squares* and has over fifty television, movie, and Broadway credits from his sixty-plus year career.

Grandpa & Grandlaur's Praline Cheesecake

SERVES 8

FOR THE PRALINE TOPPING:
2 c chopped pecans
2 tbsp brown sugar
2 tbsp butter

FOR THE CHEESECAKE:
1 (18.25-ounce) pkg yellow cake mix
1 stick (½ c) butter, melted
4 eggs, divided
2 (8-oz) pkg cream cheese
1 tsp vanilla extract
½ (3¾ c) box confectioners' sugar

Preheat oven to 350°F.

Make the topping: In a sauté pan over medium-high heat, mix together pecans, brown sugar, and butter together, cooking a few minutes to coat pecans. Remove from heat and set aside.

Make the cheesecake: Grease an oblong-sized pan. In a large bowl, mix together yellow cake mix, butter, and 1 egg together. Press into prepared pan.

In a large bowl, add remaining 3 eggs, cream cheese, vanilla extract, and confectioners' sugar together, blending until smooth with an electric mixture. Pour cream cheese mixture over cake mixture in pan.

Place cheesecake in oven, and bake for 10 minutes. Remove from oven, and top cheesecake with praline topping.

Note: For pumpkin praline cheesecake, substitute the yellow cake mix for a spice cake mix and add a small (12-oz) can of pumpkin pie filling to the cream cheese mixture.

I've had dinner with some of the most famous luminaries in the world, in some of the finest restaurants—most of the great ones you could name—but there's nothing like having dinner with my wife, my children, and my grandchildren. I found a harvest table many years ago in North Dakota. It seats twelve comfortably, but with four children and eleven grandchildren, we leak into the den. Everyone gathers around and looks forward to Grandpa and Grandlaur's Praline Cheesecake fresh from the oven.

ROBERT BENTLEY

Robert Bentley is the governor of Alabama and has held the office since 2011.

Blueberry Supreme

SERVES 10 TO 12

1 quart fresh blueberries, rinsed and patted dry
1 (20-oz) can crushed pineapple
1 (18.25-oz) pkg yellow cake mix
1½ sticks (¾ c) butter, melted

Preheat oven to 350°F.

In a large bowl, combine all the ingredients, and stir until well-mixed.

Pour batter into a 9- by 13-inch baking dish and bake in preheated oven for 35 to 40 minutes until the top of cake is golden brown. Remove from oven, cool and serve.

As an adult, Blueberry Supreme remains my favorite dessert.

Chris Branstad

Chris Branstad is the former First Lady of Iowa. Her husband, Terry Branstad, held the governor's office from 1983–1999.

Grandma Hazel's Sugar Cookies

MAKES ABOUT 3 DOZEN COOKIES

4 c all-purpose flour
1 tsp cream of tartar
1 tsp baking soda
½ tsp salt
2 sticks (1 c) butter, softened
1 c confectioners' sugar
1½ c granulated sugar, divided
1 c canola oil
2 eggs
1 tsp vanilla

In a large bowl, sift the flour, cream of tartar, baking soda, and salt together.

In a large bowl, add butter, confectioners' sugar, and 1 cup granulated sugar. Use an electric mixer and cream together. Add the oil, eggs, and vanilla, mixing to combine. Then, gradually mix in sifted dry ingredients. Chill dough for 3 to 4 hours until firm.

Preheat oven to 350°F.

Shape into walnut-sized balls and roll each ball in ½ cup granulated sugar. Place cookies on an ungreased cookie sheet. Dip the bottom of a glass in granulated sugar and press the glass onto each ball to flatten them.

Bake in preheated oven for 12 minutes, or until lightly browned. Remove cookies from cookie sheets, and cool on paper towels.

This is my husband, Terry's, grandmother's recipe and is one of our favorites. I have made them for bake sales, silent auctions, and just for the kids and grandkids to enjoy. These are not your standard cut-out sugar cookies. They are easy and taste the best of any we have ever eaten. Hazel was a marvelous cook. She could feed a crowd with one chicken and some vegetables out of her garden! She taught me how to make apple pie but, like many women of her generation, she never used a recipe. She passed away at ninety-one, but the whole Branstad family will always remember her wonderful food and hospitality.

Wicked Good Pumpkin Whoopie Pies with Cream Cheese Filling

MAKES ABOUT 2 DOZEN

FOR THE WHOOPIE PIE:
2 c packed brown sugar
1 c vegetable oil
1 (15-oz) can pumpkin purée
2 eggs
1 tsp vanilla extract
3 c all-purpose flour
1 tsp cinnamon
1 tsp baking soda
1 tsp baking powder
1 tsp salt

FOR THE CREAM CHEESE FILLING:
½ stick (¼ c) unsalted butter, softened
1 (8-oz) pkg cream cheese, softened
1 lb confectioners' sugar
2 tsp. vanilla extract
½ tsp salt

Preheat oven to 350°F. Line 2 cookie sheets with parchment paper.

In a large mixing bowl, combine brown sugar and oil, mixing until well-incorporated. Add pumpkin purée, eggs, and vanilla, and beat with an electric mixer until well-combined.

In a separate bowl, combine the dry ingredients, adding flour, cinnamon, baking soda, baking powder, and salt. Stir to combine. Add the dry ingredients to the pumpkin mixture slowly, making sure that the dry ingredients are well-incorporated and that the batter is lump-free.

Drop dough onto prepared cookie sheet using a tablespoon or small cookie scoop, with about a 2-inch space between dough. (You should fit 12 on each cookie sheet.) Bake in preheated oven for 10 minutes or until a toothpick stuck in center of cake comes out clean. Remove from oven, and let cool completely before frosting.

Make the filling: In a large bowl, add butter and cream cheese. Beat with electric mixer on medium speed until both butter and cream cheese are well-blended. Add vanilla extract and salt.

Put mixer on lowest speed setting, slowly adding the confectioners' sugar. Be careful not to turn the mixer on too high too soon or the sugar will fly everywhere. Once the sugar has been well-incorporated, turn the mixer to medium-high and beat until fluffy, about 2 minutes.

Frost the flat portion of one pumpkin cake with the cream cheese icing using a spatula. Take another pumpkin cake and sandwich them together. Repeat process until all whoopie pies are assembled. Serve.

Alan Muraoka

Alan Muraoka is an actor and theater director. He's known for his role on *Sesame Street*.

My in-laws live just outside of Portland, Maine, in a quaint little town called Gorham. The first time I went up there I was introduced to a whoopie pie, which consists of two small, round cakes which are sandwiched together with a creamy filling. The traditional whoopie pie consists of chocolate cake with a sweet filling made from shortening and powdered sugar. This is my riff on the original, using a pumpkin cake as the base and a cream cheese filling, which I much prefer over the original filling.

Christine Brennan

Christine Brennan is an American sports columnist best known for her Olympic figure skating reporting.

The Brennan Family Chocolate Chip Cookies

MAKES ABOUT 3½ DOZEN COOKIES

2¼ c all-purpose flour
1 tsp baking soda
1 tsp salt
2 sticks (1 c) butter, softened
¾ c granulated sugar
¾ c packed brown sugar
1 tsp vanilla extract
2 large eggs
1 c chocolate chips, plus another cup if you want more

Preheat oven to 375°F.

In a small bowl, combine flour, baking soda, and salt. Set aside.

In a large bowl, combine butter, granulated sugar, and brown sugar. Mix with an electric mixer until creamy, and then add the vanilla. Add eggs, one at a time, beating well after each addition. Gradually add the dry ingredients, mixing to incorporate. Then, stir in the chocolate chips. Drop dough by rounded tablespoon onto ungreased cooking sheets.

Bake for 9 to 11 minutes or until golden brown. Cool on cookie sheets for 2 minutes, and then serve.

I'm not much of an experienced cook, so I'm submitting a favorite family recipe for chocolate chip cookies. These cookies are easy, delicious (cooked and uncooked), and fun to bake with the family. We've been baking these through many generations of moms. This recipe is close to my heart and brings back many happy, family times.

DEB MCLEAN

Deb McLean is the Nutrition Director of the Community Meals Program at Somerville-Cambridge Elder Service in Massachusetts.

Zucchini Chocolate Chip Cookies

MAKES 4 DOZEN

1¼ c flour
¾ c light brown sugar
¼ tsp baking soda
½ tsp salt
¼ c canola oil
1 egg (if substituting egg, add 1 tbsp oil)
1 tsp vanilla extract
1 c grated zucchini (from 1 small zucchini)
½ c semi-sweet chocolate morsels

Preheat oven to 375°F. Prepare cookie sheets by lightly oiling them.

In a large bowl, mix the flour, sugar, baking soda, and salt. Add the wet ingredients—canola oil, egg, and extract, mixing by hand until well-blended. Stir in grated zucchini, mixing to moisten the batter. Add chocolate chips, stirring to combine.

Drop cookie mixture onto cookie sheet by rounded teaspoon, 2 inches apart.

Bake cookies for 10 to 12 minutes or until brown in preheated oven. Remove cookies to wire racks to cool.

BIG BIRD

Big Bird is the star of *Sesame Street*.

Granny Bird's Scrumptious Rainbow Parfait

SERVES 4

3 c sliced colorful fruits (strawberries, blueberries, bananas, peaches, kiwi, etc.)
3 graham crackers
2 c low-fat plain or vanilla-flavored yogurt
2 tbsp sunflower seeds (optional)
Clear plastic cups

Mix the fruit together in a bowl.

Place graham crackers in a sealed plastic bag and crush with a rolling pin.

Spoon layers of fruit, yogurt, and graham cracker crumbs (in any order) in each clear cup. If you'd like, sprinkle sunflower seeds on top. Serve.

Hi, friends! It's Big Bird from Sesame Street! I love spending time with my Granny Bird. When I go to her house, we love to cook together. I'd like to share a very special recipe that she taught me. This Rainbow Parfait is a perfect snack or dessert. It's healthy, colorful, and so much fun to make! I like to help Granny Bird by mixing the fruits together, then layering all of the ingredients. It's fun to make a pattern like yogurt, fruit, yogurt, fruit. Try to make a rainbow of different colored fruits—the more colorful the better! We birds like to sprinkle some sunflower seeds on top for an extra crunch. Granny Bird and I hope you enjoy making and eating this Rainbow Parfait as much as we do!

JOSH FRIEDLAND

Josh Friedland is a food writer and editor, who writes the award-winning blog, The Food Section, and has written for the *New York Times* and the *Washington Post*.

Papa's Mandelbrot

MAKES APPROXIMATELY 24 COOKIES

3 eggs
1 c sugar
½ c canola oil
1 tsp vanilla extract
1 c almonds, blanched (skins removed) and roughly chopped
2½ c flour
1 tsp baking powder

In a medium mixing bowl, beat together the eggs, sugar, oil, and vanilla until well-blended.

In a large mixing bowl, combine nuts, flour, and baking powder and mix together.

Add the egg mixture to the dry ingredients, mixing well with a spatula. Cover the bowl with plastic wrap and refrigerate for 3 hours.

Preheat oven to 350°F. Remove the dough from the bowl and form into two log-like loafs on a parchment-covered baking sheet. The width of each section will be the length of your cookie, so if you want long cookies, make them wide, but if you prefer a smaller cookie, make them narrow.

Bake in the preheated oven for 25 minutes. Remove from the oven and slice the logs width-wise into 1-inch wide cookies.

Lay the slices down on the baking sheet and bake for another 15 minutes (or until golden brown). Flip them over and repeat on the other side. Remove the cookies to a rack and wait for them to cool before eating.

A direct translation of mandelbrot from Yiddish would be "almond bread," but these hard, crunchy, nutty cookies might be better understood as Jewish biscotti. Like their Italian cookie cousins, they are twice-baked (first, as log-like loaves, and then cut into slices browned on each side) and excellent dunked into a hot mug of coffee or tea. The simple dough may be amalgamated with dried fruit, chocolate chips, or spices, but I prefer my grandfather Saul's traditional recipe where chunks of almonds reign supreme. They were a staple of his baking repertoire, which took off after he retired and continued into his nineties. He seemed to always have an endless supply in his freezer, which he would lay out on a plate when setting the table so that they would defrost just in time for dessert. You can also store them in an airtight container for a week or so, though they may lose a bit of their crunch after a few days, if they even last that long.

Barbara Bush

Barbara Bush is the former First Lady of the United States.

Baked Peaches Flambé

MAKES ABOUT 12 SERVINGS

4 (24-oz) cans peach halves, drained, liquid reserved
Juice from 1 lemon
1 c firmly-packed brown sugar
1 cinnamon stick, broken in half
2 tbsp vanilla extract
4 tbsp unsalted butter, cut into small pieces
½ c brandy
Whipping cream, slightly whipped

Preheat oven to 250°F.

Place peaches cut-side-down in a 13- by 9-inch glass baking dish, arranging in a tight layer. Set aside.

Pour reserved peach liquid into a medium saucepan and add lemon juice, brown sugar, cinnamon stick, and vanilla, and bring to a boil over medium-high heat. Cook until sugar dissolves, about 2 minutes. Remove cinnamon sticks and pour juice over peaches. Rearrange peaches in neat rows, if needed.

Top each peach half with butter and bake in preheated oven for 1 hour, or until the liquid has reduced to a thick syrupy sauce. Remove from oven and cool to room temperature.

To serve, place baking dish on trivet and pour brandy over peaches. Carefully light brandy with a long-stemmed match. Use a serving spoon to divide peaches among dessert plates (2 per serving), spooning still flaming syrup over peaches. Serve with whipped cream.

Susan Anton

Susan Anton is an actress, singer, and former Miss America contestant. She appeared on *Baywatch* and as the host of the "Great Radio City Music Hall Spectacular."

Apple Brown Betty

SERVES 8

6 tbsp unsalted butter, cut into pieces, divided
2½ lb Granny Smith apples, peeled, cored, and sliced about ¼-inch thick
1 tbsp freshly squeezed lemon juice
1¼ c stale plain cake crumbs (such as sponge cake, pound cake, or angel food cake) or soft fresh breadcrumbs
½ c light brown sugar
¼ c granulated sugar
1¼ tsp ground cinnamon
¼ tsp ground allspice
¼ tsp ground ginger
Pinch of ground cloves
Pinch of salt
⅓ c apple cider
Vanilla ice cream, to serve

Preheat the oven to 375°F. Generously coat a 1½-quart shallow baking dish with 1 tablespoon butter.

In a large bowl, toss apples and lemon juice together.

In a small bowl, combine cake crumbs, brown sugar, granulated sugar, cinnamon, allspice, ginger, cloves, and salt and toss until well-mixed.

Scatter 3 tablespoons of the crumb mixture onto the bottom of the baking dish and top with half of the apples. Drizzle the apple cider over the apples then top with about half of the remaining crumb mixture. Dot with half of the remaining butter. Repeat with the remaining fruit, crumbs, and butter.

Bake in the preheated oven until the apples are bubbly and tender and the crumbs are nicely browned, 45 to 50 minutes. Cool briefly on a wire cooling rack before serving warm, with scoops of ice cream on top.

Cooking has always been one of the great joys of my life. When I was a young girl, I was constantly looking for new ways to delight my family with my latest culinary creation. Sweets were a surefire hit, so I was always on the lookout for a yummy new recipe, preferably one that involved apples. You see, I grew up on my grandfather's apple ranch in southern California, so apples were plentiful and delicious. I love this recipe because it requires only a few ingredients, is quick, and super easy. Add a scoop of your favorite vanilla ice cream and you have a perfect way to say "I love you." Enjoy!

Bradley Ogden

Award-winning Chef Bradley Ogden is the genius behind such restaurants as One Market in San Francisco, Fish Story, and Bradley Ogden (in Las Vegas). His honors include "Chef of the Year" by the Culinary Institute of America and "Restaurant of the Year" by the James Beard Foundation.

Apple Crumb Pie

From *Holiday Dinners with Bradley Ogden* (Running Press, 2011)

SERVES 8

FOR THE PIE:
7 to 8 cooking apples, like Granny Smith or Pippin
1 tbsp lemon juice
2 tbsp all-purpose flour
½ c sugar
¼ tsp freshly grated cinnamon

FOR THE CRUMB TOPPING:
½ c granulated sugar
½ c firmly-packed light brown sugar
¾ c all-purpose flour
¼ tsp ground ginger
¼ tsp ground nutmeg
1 tsp ground cinnamon
Pinch of salt
¼ tsp lemon zest
6 tbsp unsalted butter, chilled and cut into pieces
1 refrigerated pie crust

Peel and core the apples. Slice the apples about ¼-inch thick (strive for 6 or 7 cups of apple slices) and toss the apple slices with the lemon juice.

In a large bowl, mix the flour, sugar, and cinnamon. (Use more or less sugar depending on your taste and the sweetness of the apples.) Toss the sugar mixture with the apples and set aside.

Prepare the crumb topping: In a medium bowl, stir together the sugars, flour, spices, salt, and lemon zest. Cut in the butter with a fork or a pastry blender until the pieces of butter are the size of oatmeal. Chill until assembling the pie.

Preheat oven to 375°F.

Roll pie crust on a lightly-floured surface to about ⅛-inch thick. Fold lightly into quarters and unfold into a 9-inch glass pie plate. Trim off excess dough to about ½-inch larger than the edge of the pie plate. Turn the ½-inch of dough under the edge and press a decorative trim with your thumb and forefinger.

Pile the apples in the dough, leaving them higher in the center. Sprinkle about half of the crumb topping on top of the apples. Bake for 20 minutes in preheated oven, then add the remaining topping and continue baking for another 40 minutes, or until the apples become tender. Remove from oven, let cool, and serve.

This is an updated version of my Grandmother Eve's apple pie that I remember growing up as a kid in Michigan. It's a wonderfully delicious apple pie graced with a simple yet flavorful crunchy crumb topping. Use Granny Smith or Pippin apples for this recipe. Recipe from Holiday Dinners with Bradley Ogden, *published by Running Press, 2011.*

Lisa Sharples

Lisa Sharples is the president of allrecipes.com, one of the largest food websites featuring thousands of free recipes created by home cooks.

This sour cherry pie recipe is so simple to make that I can put it together and get it in the oven in less than 10 minutes. The hardest thing about this pie is tracking down canned sour cherries, but if you look carefully, you can find them in most grocery stores. When the pie is served, top with vanilla ice cream to add the element of sweet to the sour!

My father used this recipe when I was growing up, and it was always one of my family's favorites. Now that I'm grown with six kids of my own, I realize why it was my dad's go-to party dessert—it's delicious and it only takes minutes to put it together. Once when I needed to prepare a dozen sour cherry pies for a bake sale, my husband timed me while I made each to see how fast I could make them. By the twelfth pie, I had gotten my preparation time down to 1 minute per pie, lattice crust and all!

At allrecipes.com, Thanksgiving is a huge event with more than 20 million busy cooks visiting the site for recipes, cooking tips, and food videos. We prepare this pie every year during our live Thanksgiving how-to cooking webcast, since this is the perfect pie recipe for busy moms cooking for a crowd. The pie is a simple take on the classic cherry pie with sour cherries instead of cherry pie filling, and tapioca to sweeten it up. It's quick, delicious and sure to wow the crowd!

Sour Cherry Pie

SERVES 8

1 (15-oz) pkg double crust ready-to-use pie crust
3 (15-oz) cans pitted sour cherries, drained
3 tbsp quick-cooking tapioca
1½ c sugar
¼ tsp almond extract

Preheat oven to 400°F.

Press one of the pie crusts into a 9-inch pie plate. In a large bowl, stir together the cherries, tapioca, sugar, and almond extract in a bowl. Let the mixture stand for 3 to 5 minutes.

Meanwhile, cut the other pie crust into ½-inch strips to make a lattice top. Pour the cherry mixture into the pie shell. Lay the strips across the pie in a lattice pattern, and pinch the edges to seal.

Bake in the preheated oven 40 to 50 minutes until the crust is golden brown. Allow to cool before serving.

Nolan Smith

Nolan Smith currently plays in the NBA for the Portland Trail Blazers and was a member of the 2010 Duke University national champion team.

Grandma's Lemon Meringue Pie

SERVES 8

2¼ c sugar, divided
½ c cornstarch
2 c water
½ tsp grated lemon zest
Pinch of salt
6 large eggs, separated
½ c freshly squeezed lemon juice
1 (9-inch) baked and cooled pie crust

Preheat oven to 375°F.

In a heavy-bottomed pot over medium heat, add 1½ c sugar, cornstarch, and water, whisking together to combine. Stir in lemon zest and salt. Cook, stirring frequently, until thickened. Set aside to cool slightly.

In a small bowl, beat egg yolks and lemon juice together. Pour egg mixture into cooled cornstarch mixture. Return pot to medium heat, stirring constantly, for about 1 minute. Remove from heat and set aside to allow filling to cool completely.

Pour cooled filling into prepared pie crust. Beat egg whites in bowl of an electric mixer until soft peaks form. Gradually add remaining ¾ cup sugar with mixer running and mix until egg whites form stiff peaks. Spread meringue evenly over pie filling and bake until meringue is golden brown, about 12 to 15 minutes.

I chose this dessert because it is one dish that I remember almost rushing through meals for, actually eating all my vegetables, just so I could get this first slice after dinner!

Aran Goyoaga

Aran Goyoaga is a food stylist and photographer. Aran documents her life and work at cannellevanille.com. Her first cookbook, *Small Plates and Sweet Treats—My Family's Journey to Gluten-Free Cooking*, will be published by Little, Brown and Company in October 2012.

Quinoa Milk Pudding with Macerated Summer Berries

SERVES 4 TO 6

1 c quinoa
3 c whole milk
1 c heavy cream
¼ c plus 1 tbsp sugar, divided
Pinch of salt
1 vanilla bean, split lengthwise and seeds scraped
1 c diced strawberries
Chopped pistachios, as needed

Place the quinoa in a strainer and rinse under cold water for a few seconds.

In a medium saucepan, combine milk, cream, ¼ cup sugar, and salt, plus vanilla bean and its seeds. Bring to a simmer over medium heat. Add the quinoa and stir. Reduce heat to medium-low, cover the pot, and cook for 30 minutes while stirring occasionally. If skin starts to form on top of the milk, just stir it back in. The milk will reduce and thicken.

Ladle the mixture into bowls or jars and let it cool to room temperature. Then transfer to refrigerator and chill for about 30 minutes.

In a bowl, add strawberries and sprinkle with 1 tablespoon sugar. Toss them and let them sit at room temperature for 30 minutes until they release their juices.

Serve the puddings with the macerated strawberries and chopped pistachios.

One of the first desserts I learned to make with my mother and grandmother was arroz con leche, which translates into rice with milk. It is our version of the classic rice pudding. The smell of simmering milk and vanilla would permeate the entire house and, to this day, it is the scent I look forward to when I am in need of some comfort. This is a slight variation of that recipe using quinoa. High in protein and full of nutrients, quinoa has become a staple in our family. Served with sugar-macerated berries and chopped pistachios, this is my family's old-time favorite dessert.

Judi Dench

Judi Dench is an Academy Award and Golden Globe-winning actress known for *Shakespeare in Love* and *Chocolat*.

Bread & Butter Pudding

SERVES 8

4 tbsp butter, softened
½ (26.2-oz) Panettone cake
1 tbsp finely chopped candied lemon or orange peel
¼ c currants or raisins
1 c milk
¼ c heavy cream
Zest of half a small lemon
¼ c sugar
3 eggs, lightly beaten
Pinch of freshly grated nutmeg

Heat oven to 350°F. Butter a 1-quart baking dish.

Slice the Panettone and butter each slice. Line the bottom of the prepared baking dish with cake slices. Sprinkle with the candied peel and half the currants. Add another layer of buttered cake and sprinkle with the remaining currants.

In a large bowl, combine the milk and cream together. Stir in the lemon zest, sugar, and eggs, whisking together to combine. Pour custard mixture over the Panettone and sprinkle with nutmeg.

Bake in preheated oven until custard is set in the center, 30 to 40 minutes. Serve warm.

This is delicious and provides the perfect solution for what to do with those dry Italian cakes you receive at Christmas.

Karri Turner

Karri Turner is an actress, best known for her role on *JAG*.

Tipsy Bread Pudding

SERVES 4 TO 6

½ lb loaf Italian or French bread, cut into 1-inch cubes
2 c of milk
2 eggs, lightly beaten
¾ c packed light brown sugar
½ c golden raisins
1 tbsp vanilla extract
4 tbsp butter
½ c granulated sugar
¼ c heavy cream
2 tbsp Jack Daniels®

Preheat the oven to 325°F. Generously butter a 9-inch square pan.

Place the bread in a large bowl. Pour milk over the bread and let set for 10 to 15 minutes, until bread is soggy. In a medium bowl, mix eggs, brown sugar, raisins, and vanilla together and then stir into the bread mixture. Pour into the prepared pan and bake 20 to 25 minutes, until the pudding is set.

While the pudding bakes, prepare the sauce. Heat the butter, sugar, and cream in a heavy saucepan over medium heat until the sugar dissolves. Bring to a boil, reduce the heat, and simmer for 5 minutes. Remove from the heat and stir in the Jack Daniels.® Pour the bourbon sauce over the hot pudding. Serve warm or chilled.

Just out of a very strict college environment, I was looking for any reason to partake in bourbon. Jack Daniels® is a lifelong pal, incorporated into this fun, easy dessert. I like to serve this bread pudding warm, sometimes with a bit of whipped cream, or ice cream if you are feeling frisky. I serve it with a glass of milk . . . or a bit more Jack Daniels® straight up.

Leslie & Tony Curtis' Lemon Soufflé with Raspberry Sauce

From *Recipes for Life* (Vanguard Press, 2011)

SERVES 6

FOR THE LEMON SOUFFLÉ:
5 egg yolks
1½ c sugar
Zest and juice of 4 large lemons
2 (.25-oz) pkg unflavored gelatin
½ c room-temperature water
2 c heavy whipping cream
6 egg whites
⅛ tsp salt
⅛ tsp cream of tartar

FOR THE RASPBERRY SAUCE:
2 c raspberries, divided
2 tbsp sugar
1 tsp freshly squeezed lemon juice

Prepare a double boiler. In the top of the double boiler over gently simmering water, add egg yolks, sugar, lemon zest, and lemon juice, beating together and stirring constantly, until the mixture has thickened enough to coat a spoon. (This will take a little time.) Remove from heat. Transfer the lemon mixture to a large bowl.

In a small bowl, soak the gelatin in water. Stir to mix. Then, add the gelatin to the warm lemon mixture and stir to blend well. Set aside to cool.

When the lemon mixture is at room temperature, whip the cream with electric mixer until soft peaks form. Fold whipped cream into the lemon mixture.

In a large bowl, add, egg whites, salt ,and cream of tartar, and whip with electric mixer until stiff peaks form. Gently fold half of the whites into the lemon mixture, to lighten the base, and then gently fold in the other half. Pour mixture into an 8-cup soufflé dish.

Refrigerate at least 4 hours.

Make the raspberry sauce. Add 1½ cups raspberries to a food processor, and purée. Strain raspberry purée through a fine-mesh sieve to remove seeds. Transfer to a medium bowl, and mix in the sugar and lemon juice.

Mash the remaining ½ cup berries with a fork and stir into the puréed berry mixture. Refrigerate for at least an hour to chill through, and serve cold.

Serve lemon soufflé with raspberry sauce.

Linda Evans

Linda Evans is a television actress, best known for her roles in *The Big Valley* and *Dynasty*.

Tony and Leslie Curtis were regulars at our house in Malibu, and we shared many great dinners with them at their beautiful home in Bel Air. Being a lemon lover, I asked them for this recipe, and I've made it many times with great success. Recipe from Recipes for Life *by Linda Evans, published by Vanguard Press, 2011.*

MARILYN POLLACK NARON

Marilyn Pollack Naron is a food writer and the blogger behind SimmerTillDone.com, which has been featured on PaulaDeen.com, Sauveur, and Babble.com.

Aunt Rose (Aunt Ruth's?) Noodle Kugel

SERVES 24

1 (16-oz) pkg wide egg noodles, cooked, drained and cooled
4 eggs
½ c sour cream
1 lb cottage cheese
½ c milk
1 stick (½ c) butter, melted
¾ c sugar, as needed
1 tbsp cinnamon
1 small can crushed pineapple, drained (optional)
1 c raisins, golden raisins preferred (optional)
Extra cinnamon-sugar mixture, for sprinkling

Preheat oven to 350°F. Coat a 9- by 13-inch baking dish with baking spray.

Add noodles to a large bowl. In a separate bowl, whisk together eggs, sour cream, cottage cheese, milk, and butter. Incorporate noodles into egg mixture, mixing together to incorporate.

In a small bowl, combine sugar and cinnamon. Add most of the cinnamon-sugar mixture to noodles, tossing to coat. If you are adding the optional pineapple and raisins—and let me add it's delicious to do so—toss them in now.

Place noodle mixture into prepared pan, and sprinkle top with extra cinnamon sugar. Bake until the top is lightly browned, 45 minutes to 1 hour. Cool until safe to handle, then cut into squares and serve warm. Leftovers freeze and reheat well.

Noodle kugel is a humble dish with an outsize name—a funny name, good for comedians, grandmas, and giggling kids. Kugel is ripe with pronunciation—kooo-gle or kuh-gel or whatever, it all translates to "pass-me-that-right-now." Kugel equals golden noodles bound by sour cream and eggs, cottage cheese and sugar, dotted with fat raisins and cut into thick and improbably square slabs. It's commonly found on Jewish holiday tables and in deli case pyramids, but my family's kugel is found on a 3- by 5-inch card.

Wearing butter stains and cinnamon age spots, the card appears each holiday in my mother's kitchen—first under a fridge magnet ("I need to know where it is") and eventually, on the counter. My mom could probably make kugel in her sleep, but the card sits there, near the Pyrex, guiding the process like a curious lucky charm.

Most Jewish families pass down a kugel recipe and inevitably a kugel family secret, some earnest addition like peaches or carrots or even chocolate chips. Kugel lovers divide into sweet or savory, and at least in the matter of kugel, I stand with the sweet. I like my kugel luscious, sugared, and cheesy, with distinct overtones of blintzes and dessert.

My mom received the Selectric-typed card long ago from Aunt Rose, as dear a lady as there ever was, and it was fondly known as Aunt Rose's Kugel for decades, right up to the shocking family moment when it was revealed to be Aunt Ruth's. My Grandma Trudy had three sisters—Ruth, Rose, and Florence—and all four lived near each other, wore curlers, shopped sales, and checked in by phone before ten. The four Weinstock girls—actually "LaVin," the name lost at Ellis Island—were bound by love so fierce that it often excluded their husbands but extended monumentally, and quite judgmentally, to each other. At one time or another, they all baked and served this kugel.

Florence and Rose were the better cooks—my grandma never met a Cantonese takeout menu she didn't like—and though Rose's dish may be as sweet as Ruth's, there was, of course, satisfaction in setting the recipe record straight. Enjoy noodling around on your own, and repeat the motto with me—never attribute a kugel to the wrong sister.

Acknowledgments

This book would not have been possible without the loving hands that guided us through this very exciting, but scary world of publishing. And so, I lovingly thank:

Jean Sagendorph for her literary genius and advice and for calling our office about something totally different, but listening to an idea that we thought could work. It did. Thanks, Jean.

Glenn Yeffeth for chutzpah and a belief that good publishing and doing good are not mutually exclusive.

Jennifer Canzoneri, Lindsay Marshall and all the patient folks at BenBella. You never let on that our lack of experience might have been a tad frustrating at times.

Paula Breen, Leigh Camp, Wendy Simard, and Adrienne Lang.

Elliot Jacobson for his incredible friendship, mentoring, and rolodex. You have more friends than anyone I've ever known. Count me twice; you mean that much to me.

Thanks to all of you who helped find us these terrific folks who gave so generously of their time to submit recipes and stories for this book:

Michael Flynn
Peggy Ingraham
Erika Kelly
Jim Maglione
John Maroon
RoseMary Regalbuto
Neil Romano
Daryl Twerdahl

Thanks too, to Jessica Harrington for this crazy idea in the first place.

Thanks to my trusted army at MOWAA for putting up with a kvetching boss throughout the whole process, with special plaudits to Bob Herbolsheimer for legal work, Christopher Palazio for keeping me sane, and Liz Doyle for a fine eye for detail.

Thanks to Lindsay Garrett for some of the most incredible food photos ever shot and some long rides and long days taking those remarkable pictures.

Thanks too to my equal partner in this endeavor, Marley Rave. This was a joint effort and most of the credit goes to you. You never waver and you always remain upbeat. Yes, kiddo, we did it.

And finally, to all the people who took a leap of faith with us and submitted recipes and stories when you probably didn't even think we could pull this thing off. Well we did, and it's precisely because of you that we did. A tip of our aprons to all of you for understanding that if we are to truly end senior hunger in this country, we can't do it alone. We all must work together so no senior goes hungry™.

With gratitude and humility, this book is for all who are touched by the loving hands of Meals On Wheels.

Index

D

E

F

G

H

I

J

K

L

M

N

T

U

W

Z